Standard Grade

English

revision notes

11/010708

The name 'Marvellous Marvelon' on page 25 is fictitious and is used for illustrative purposes only.

ISBN 978-1-898890-37-9

Published by
Leckie & Leckie Ltd, 3rd floor, 4 Queen Street, Edinburgh, EH2 1JE
Tel: 0131 220 6831 Fax: 0131 225 9987
enquiries@leckieandleckie.co.uk
www.leckieandleckie.co.uk

Edited by Ellen Doherty

Thanks to
Emily Dewhurst (production assistance), Margaret McKay and Rosemary Macrae (proofreading), Caleb Rutherford (design) and Hamish Sanderson (page make-up and illustration).

Thanks also to
Faber and Faber Limited for permission to reproduce Preludes (i) from Collected Poems 1909–1962 by T.S. Eliot on page 16; to Gillon Aitken Associates for permission to reproduce the extract from Bad Land by Jonathan Raban on page 23 (Copyright © Jonathan Raban 1996); and to the Scottish Qualifications Authority for permission to reproduce extracts from previous exam papers on pages 29 and 61. Every effort has been made to contact all the copyright holders. If any have been inadvertently overlooked, the publishers will be pleased to make the necessary arrangements for them.

A CIP Catalogue record for this book is available from the British Library.

Leckie & Leckie is a division of Huveaux plc

CONTENTS

INTRODUCTION

Course Content

Standard Grade English is a two-year course during which you will develop your skills in Reading, Writing and Talking.

During the course you will:

- **read** short passages and longer works for comprehension
- **write** pieces for your folio (the five major pieces of work you produce during your course)
- **present** Individual Talks and **participate** in Group Discussions.

Although they sound as though they are separate skills, Reading, Writing and Talking are interrelated: you will read pieces of writing, you will write about reading and you will talk about both reading and writing!

Standard Grade English is presented differently in every school in Scotland. The Scottish Qualifications Authority (SQA) does not set out a specific syllabus as it does for other subjects: there is no set amount of information to learn nor specific books to read. This means you will not necessarily study the same Writing or do the same Reading or Talking as your friend in another school. Your teacher will make decisions about which texts and activities will be most appropriate for you. This way, the course is tailored especially for you.

The work in the course is divided into **units**. A unit of work could last for several weeks (for example, studying a novel or play) or might only last for one or two periods (for example, working on an aspect of Close Reading).

Assessment

Grade-related criteria

Your performance in Standard Grade English is assessed against standards (called 'grade-related criteria'). This means you are not being marked in comparison to other students in the class – your teacher is not concerned with whether you are much better than Kevin or worse than Fiona! You are being assessed on what **you** can do.

One-third each

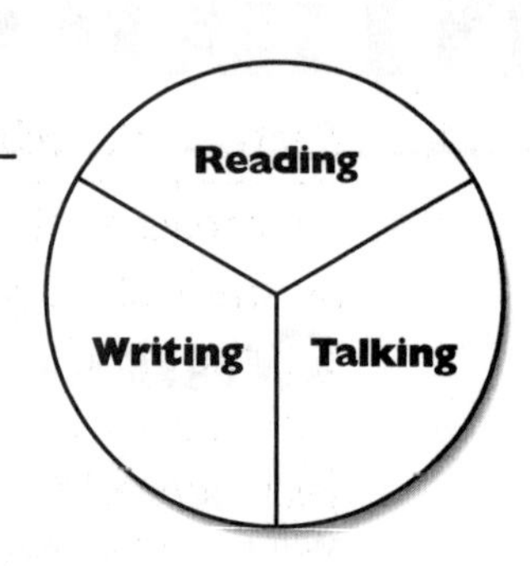

Your assessment in Standard Grade English is like a cake:

- one slice (⅓) of the cake is your grade for Reading
- one slice (⅓) of the cake is your grade for Writing
- one slice (⅓) of the cake is your grade for Talking.

Each slice is called an **element**.

Assessment of your Reading

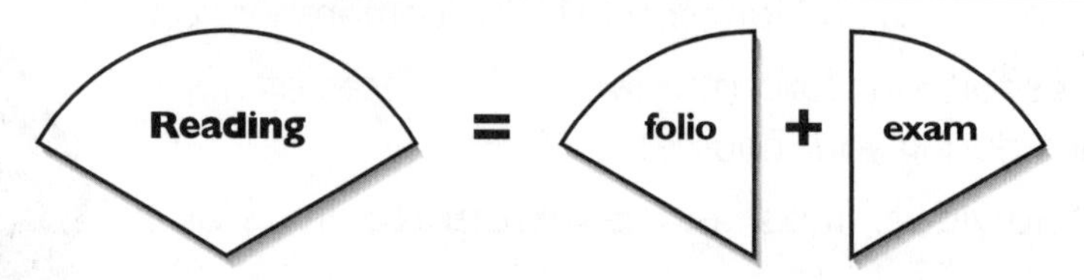

The Reading element of your course is assessed in two ways:

- by your folio work
- by your performance in the end-of-course Reading exam.

Your Reading work is assessed by external markers (SQA markers from outside your school). One marker marks your folio work and another marker marks your exam.

Assessment of your Writing

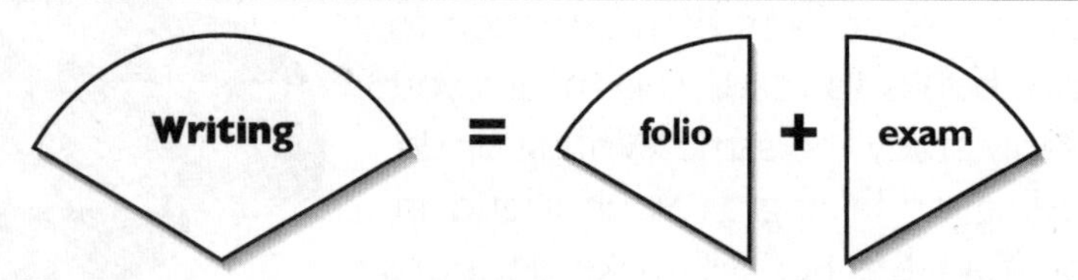

The Writing element of your course is assessed in the same ways as the Reading element:

- by your folio work
- by your performance in the end-of-course Writing exam.

Your Writing work is also assessed by external markers.

Assessment of your Talking

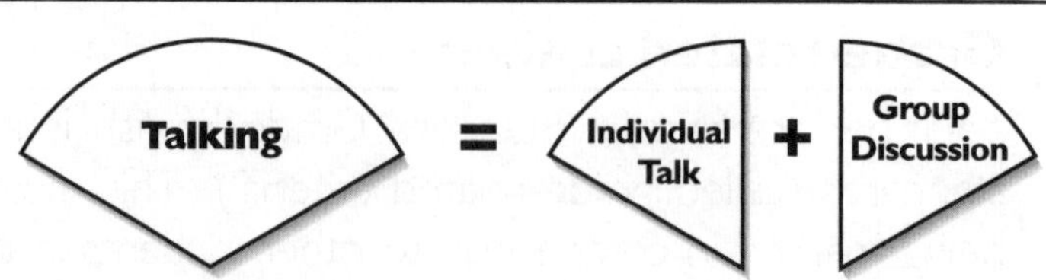

The Talking element is assessed by your teacher throughout your course. This is called **continuous assessment**. Your teacher grades your Individual Talks and your performance in Group Discussions. He/she then submits your final grade to the SQA towards the end of your fourth year.

Other continuous assessment

Your teacher also assesses the work you do in Reading and Writing during your course: he/she looks at your work and comments on it many times over the two years. He/she will then advise you which level(s) of exam papers you should take at the end of your course: Foundation, General and/or Credit. Towards the end of your fourth year, he/she will also send in a grade for your Reading and a grade for your Writing to the SQA. These are estimates of the grades your teacher expects you to achieve in the exam and are used by the SQA in the event of an appeal or other special reason.

Your Folio

Five pieces

Your folio contains the **five** major pieces of work which you produce during your course and which your teacher sends to the SQA in March of your fourth year. It contains **two** pieces of **Writing** and **three** responses to **Reading**.

Your own work

Your folio is yours: it is your responsibility to choose the pieces and to make sure they are your own work. Your teacher will help and advise you – he/she will comment on your work at various stages. However, you must not ask or expect your teacher or anyone else to help you write any part of your folio. Also, you may not copy someone else's work for it. Your folio must be **your own unaided writing**. In fact, both you and your teacher are asked to sign the folio stating that it contains only your own work.

Your best work

Your folio should not be done in a rush in February of your fourth year! The point of having nearly two years to complete your folio is that it allows you to take your time and ensure that the five pieces are your best work. You can include in your folio work you have completed in your third and/or fourth year.

Handwritten or typed?

Your folio may be handwritten or produced on a computer, word-processor or a typewriter. You may have heard that you will get better marks if you type your work – this is not true! The marker is interested in the quality of your work and not whether it is handwritten or not. Of course, if your handwriting is very untidy and difficult to read, you will have to think about how best to present your work – typing may be a solution if you have access to the equipment you need.

How long?

One frequently asked question is 'How long do the pieces for my folio have to be?' The SQA states that the 'length must be appropriate to the purpose'. So, if you are writing a poem, your piece may be quite short; if you are writing the story of your life, it may be quite long! In other words, **your purpose will determine how much you should write**.

At Foundation level, 100 words is the minimum requirement for **Reading** pieces. It is best to try to write more than 100 words if at all possible. A marker cannot judge how well you can write if you submit only one or two paragraphs. At General level, you should write between 300 and 800 words for a Reading piece. Remember, the length of your writing should be appropriate to your purpose. For Credit students, the suggested maximum is 800 words.

The same goes for **Writing** pieces. Again, there is no set length because you may include a poem which is very short or a story which is quite long. The SQA suggests that the minimum at Foundation level is 100 words. The length at General level should be appropriate to the purpose and the suggested maximum for Credit is 800 words.

Don't worry too much about these limits. A lot of students spend time counting words. It is more helpful to check whether you have fulfilled the task. For example, if you are writing an essay about issues which face young people as we enter the new millennium, you would be unlikely to fulfil the task in enough detail unless you were to write several hundred words.

Your end-of-course Exams

Your Reading exam

At the end of your course, you sit a Reading exam consisting of either one or two papers. You will sit either

- the Foundation paper only

or

- the Foundation and General papers

or

- the General and Credit papers.

Your teacher will advise you which paper(s) to sit. He/she will base this advice on your performance during the course.

If you are sitting the Foundation level paper, it is always best to sit the General level paper also. This will give you the chance to achieve a General level grade.

In each Reading paper, you read a passage of fiction or non-fiction and then answer questions on it. This type of reading is called 'Close Reading'. Each paper lasts 50 minutes.

Your Writing exam

Whatever your level, you sit the same Writing exam paper at the end of your course as all other Standard Grade students. This exam lasts 1 hour 15 minutes and contains a choice of approximately 20 essay topics about which to write. You should attempt only **one** of these. There will be a wide range from which to choose, so don't worry – you will find one that you are able to do.

Key Standard Grade Skills

To perform well in Standard Grade English, it is vital that you:

- **meet deadlines**
- **plan, draft and redraft**
- **keep organised.**

Meet deadlines

If you do not complete your folio and send it to the SQA on time, you will not be awarded a grade for Reading or Writing. This is the case even if you sit the end-of-course exams. (Remember that the grades for Reading and Writing are a combination of the folio and the exam). Similarly, if you complete your folio but do not sit the exam, you will receive no overall award.

Plan, draft and redraft

Whenever you are working on an essay in class or at home, remember to plan, draft and redraft your work. Redrafting is part of the process of writing. It would be easy if redrafting meant simply copying out your work neatly. Of course, neat presentation is important but redrafting is about looking afresh at your writing and thinking about how it could be improved: perhaps some parts are too long or too short; perhaps you want to change some words; perhaps you have decided on a different ending. Writers usually make several drafts of a piece of work, improving it at each stage.

You should **always redraft your work for your folio**. An advantage of Standard Grade English is that your final award is based not only on your performance in the exam but also on your folio work. Make the most of this advantage by ensuring your final draft of each piece of your folio work is as good as it can be.

Keep organised

You are involved in a lot of reading, writing and talking in Standard Grade English. You don't have to be super efficient, but it is a good idea to keep your drafts of Close Reading answers, Writing, notes from Group Discussions, etc in an organised way. A good start is to have three folders labelled 'Reading', 'Writing' and 'Talking'.

Your Final Certificate

The grade you receive will be on a scale from 1 to 6.

Look at the table below.

Level	*Grade*
Credit	1 or 2
General	3 or 4
Foundation	5 or 6

Your final certificate will show three grades – one for Reading, one for Writing and one for Talking. The average of these gives your overall award. Look at the example below of what this might look like.

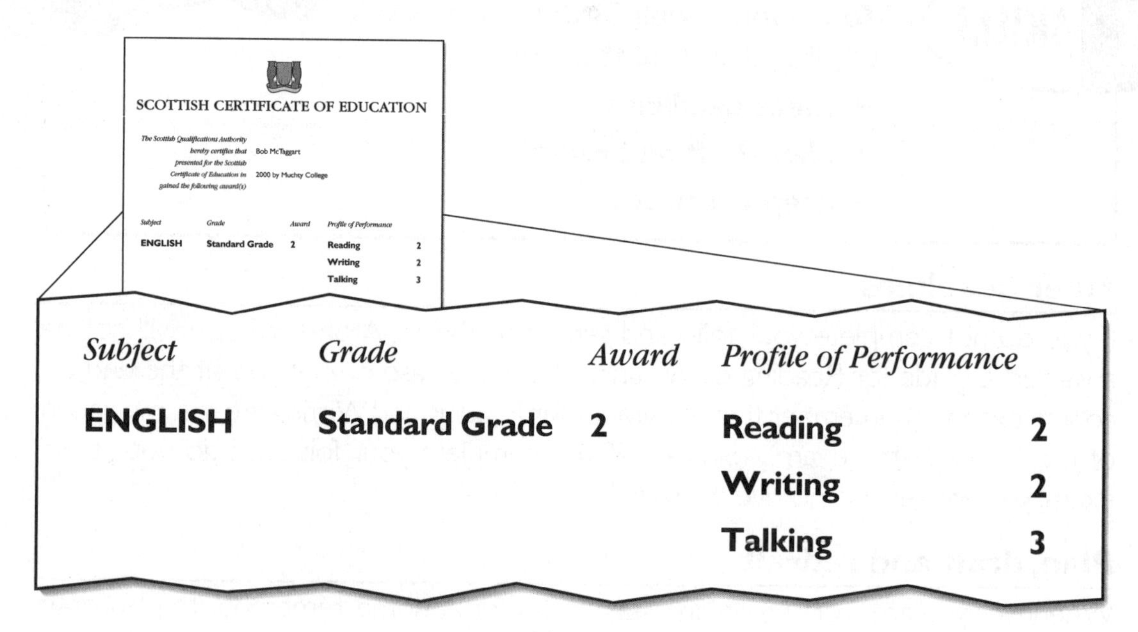

ACTION to TAKE

You will find more information about all of these aspects of Standard Grade English in the following sections of this book. Study each of these sections carefully.

Use the checklists at the end of each section to help you assess your performance in Reading, Writing and Talking.

Always check with your teacher for further details about your course.

Check it

You can find out the meanings of all the Key Words you must know for Standard Grade English on pages 78 to 80. Remember, however, to check with your teacher for a fuller description of these words and terms or for any other words about which you may be unsure.

READING

Key Reading Skills

Close Reading of Fiction

Close Reading of Non-fiction

Close Reading Exam Skills

Critical Evaluations

The Most Important Reading Skill

Critical Evaluation Checklist

KEY READING SKILLS

KEY SKILLS

During your course you will develop the skills of:
- **reading critically**
- **studying different types of writing**
- **forming your own opinions about literature**
- **giving reasons for your opinions.**

Reading critically

When you read for Standard Grade, always **analyse what you are reading**. Don't just read passively, but think about **why** the author has written in a particular way. Ask yourself, for example:

- why has the author used a certain word?
- why has he/she repeated an idea?
- what does he/she feel about the topic?
- why has he/she used such short sentences?

Reading in this way is called 'reading critically' – all this means is that you should always **think** while you read. Try to get into the habit of reading critically. It will make Standard Grade English a lot easier!

Studying different types of writing

You will read different types of writing during your course, including **prose fiction**, **poetry**, **drama**, **media** and **non-fiction prose**.

- Prose fiction includes novels and short stories.
- Poetry is composition in verse.
- Drama includes plays and scripts.
- Media includes excerpts from films, TV programmes, newspapers and advertisements.
- Non-fiction prose includes travel writing and biography.

A work of fiction is an invented story. A work of non-fiction contains purely facts and/or opinions.

Examples of fiction	***Examples of non-fiction***
Jingo, a novel by Terry Pratchett	*Elvis*, a biography by Albert Goldman
ET, a film by Steven Spielberg	*Encyclopedia Britannica*, a reference text
Eastenders, a TV programme	*Ibiza Uncovered*, a documentary
Macbeth, a play by William Shakespeare	*In India*, a piece of travel writing
Kiss Kiss, a short story by Roald Dahl	*The Scots*, a magazine article
Tulips, a poem by Sylvia Plath	*My Life*, an autobiography
Space Journey, a piece of fictional travel writing	*Scottish Team Wins Again*, a newspaper article

ACTION to TAKE

Can you think of other examples of fiction and non-fiction?

Forming your own opinions about literature

Your **personal opinions** about the literature you read (or programmes you watch) are very important. Here are two examples:

- Your friend may love *Romeo and Juliet* while you may think it is soppy and old-fashioned.
- Poetry can be romantic, angry, sad, exciting – it can involve any emotion you can think of! You may love *Daffodils*, a poem which no-one else seems to like.

Giving reasons for your opinions

When you are writing about literature, it is not enough simply to say that a text is '*brilliant*' or '*awful*'. You must also give **reasons** for your opinions. For example:

- you may watch films or TV programmes as part of your course. Some students think these are easy options to write about because they spend a lot of time watching TV programmes and talking about them with their friends! However, the same standards apply to an evaluation of a film as they do to an evaluation of a poem. You will comment in detail on aspects of the film or programme. Using technical terms, you will consider aspects of film-making (including genre, lighting, sound effects, direction and representation).

During your course you will develop these four key skills in **two** main ways:

1. You will read and analyse pieces of fiction and non-fiction in class and at home. This is called **Close Reading** – you read and then answer questions on a particular passage.
   - You could be asked questions on a short extract from, for example, a novel you are studying in class. This will help you later on if you are going to write a Critical Evaluation of this text. This kind of Close Reading is sometimes called textual analysis because you are answering questions on a short extract. It will help you to a greater understanding of the text as a whole once you have finished reading it.
   - You could also be asked questions on a short fiction or non-fiction passage you have never seen before. This is another kind of Close Reading. This is the type of exercise you have to do in the Reading part of the exam at the end of the course.

   Your teacher should give you plenty of practice in doing both these kinds of Close Reading.
2. You will write **Critical Evaluations** on texts in class and at home. A Critical Evaluation is a final piece of work which you attempt only after you have thought about the text, discussed it, answered questions on it and studied particular aspects of it. When you have done all this, you will be ready to plan, draft and then write a Critical Evaluation. You include your best three Critical Evaluations in your folio.

More Info

The rest of this chapter gives advice on how best to answer Close Reading questions and write Critical Evaluations.

CLOSE READING OF FICTION

This section will help you tackle Close Reading of the various texts which you study in class. It will also help you tackle Close Reading passages in the exam.

What will the questions ask you to do?

A Close Reading question will ask you to do one of the following:

- **give your overall impression of the text**

  A question may ask you to summarise what the text is about – to explain its overall message. For example:

  Sum up in a few words what the poem is about.

- **obtain particular information from the text**

  A question may focus on a particular section of the text. You may be asked why a poet has used a particular word or why a character behaves as he/she does, or why particular stage directions have been given.

- **grasp ideas or feelings implied in a text**

  A question may ask you to look 'behind' the words on the page. For example:

  - you may be asked what you can deduce about a character who is described as biting his nails, shuffling his feet and stuttering over his words. (You might deduce from this that he is anxious or nervous.) You may be asked to look at a character in a film and comment on what is implied about her from the way she dresses.

  It is your personal opinion about the text which counts. As long as you can find evidence for your opinions and include it in your answer, your opinions about a text are perfectly valid.

- **evaluate the writer's attitudes, assumptions and argument**

  To do this, again you look 'behind' the words. In this case, you are trying to find out what the **writer** feels about a topic. For example:

  - a writer may write a short story on the theme of prejudice in which the main character is a victim of racial discrimination but who wins her case in court. You could work out from aspects of this story – from the character, from how she behaves and speaks, from the language the writer uses, from the fact that there is a 'happy ending' – that the writer disapproves of racial discrimination. If, however, the writer uses a less sympathetic character, uses negative language and the story does not have a 'happy ending', then you might deduce that the writer approves of racial discrimination.

- **appreciate the writer's craft**

  The word 'craft' here means the **techniques** the writer uses. To answer this type of question, you identify these techniques and suggest why they have been used.

More Info

Look out for the KEY TERMS boxes later in this chapter. They tell you the correct terms to use when describing writers' techniques.

How much should you write?

Each question will normally give you an indication of how much to write as an answer. For example:

> … in a few sentences …

or

> What two points are made about …?

Alternatively, there may be marks given after each question.

Close Reading of Prose Fiction

ACTION to TAKE

Study this extract from a short story. How can you tell it is a piece of prose?

> It was a sunny week in late August, when the heat curled along the streets and up the tenement stairs of the baker's oven of a city, that Timothy Maguire came to stay with his widowed sister and his nephew.
>
> 'By God, have I not brought the good weather with me!' he exclaimed, putting down his suitcase and beaming at them, his round face shining with sweat.
>
> 'Mary!' he embraced his sister, then thrust out his hand. 'And this hulking giant cannot be young Martin?'
>
> 'I'm nineteen, Uncle Tim.' Martin's hand was gripped.
>
> 'Nineteen, is it?' Timothy whistled. 'By God, there's time passed, and a lot of Maguire grown in this lad, Mary. Does he not look like our father when young?'

'He has the eyes, just. The face is his own father's. Come, sit down.'

Timothy sat and pulled out a handkerchief to mop his face and the wet, darkened roots of his fair hair. 'And how is it with you both?' he asked.

'Martin grows up, and I grow older,' said Mary, and plucked at a lock of her hair. 'Do you see the grey?'

from *Blood* by Keith Aitchison

Aspects of Prose

You can tell this extract is a piece of prose because it has these aspects:

- it has a main **character**, Timothy Maguire, and there is a **description** of him
- there is also **setting** – we are told both time and place
- there is **action** – Timothy arrives home
- the characters use **dialogue**
- the **language** is quite simple and straightforward
- there is evidence of a **plot**. The plot means the story of what is happening.
- the **theme** might be 'home' or 'family'

  (It is difficult to tell the plot and theme from such a short extract. Working out the plot and theme will be easier for you when you read complete texts.)
- there is **imagery** – e.g. the metaphor 'the baker's oven of a city'.

You could be asked questions about any of these aspects of prose, so think hard about them while you are reading!

ACTION to TAKE

Now look at the questions. Write down your own answer before reading the model answer.

Questions with model answers

1. Is Timothy happy to be with his sister and nephew? How can you tell?

   (This question is asking you to obtain particular information from the passage.)

Timothy is happy to be with Mary and Martin. The writer shows this in a number of ways:

- The weather is described as 'sunny' and 'good', which could be seen as a metaphor for Timothy's happiness.
- Timothy is 'beaming' which shows he is smiling happily.
- The author uses exclamation marks to show Timothy is excited.
- He 'embraces' his sister and 'thrusts out' his hand which shows he is eager to greet his relations.

Notice how the answer is very clear and well organised into a list of points. The answer includes several **quotes** and an **explanation** or **analysis** of each quote. This is a good model to follow. In your answer to the next question, try to quote from the passage and analyse the quote.

2. What evidence is there that Timothy has not seen Martin for a long time?

(This question is asking you to obtain particular information from the passage.)

We know that he has not seen Martin for a long time because he is surprised at how much he has grown – 'this hulking giant'.

Note again the use of a quote and an explanation in the answer.

3. What can you deduce about the heat from the phrase 'the baker's oven of a city'?

(This question is asking you to grasp ideas or feelings implied in the text. This is a harder question because you have to interpret why the author has used a phrase and not just comment on the phrase itself.)

Because an oven is very hot and contains a concentrated amount of heat, I deduce that the city is extremely hot and airless.

4. How has the writer built up a picture of Timothy?

(This question is asking you to appreciate the writer's craft.)

The writer builds up a picture of Timothy in two main ways. He describes him – 'his round face', 'Timothy whistled'. This builds up a picture of a happy man. He also shows his character as energetic through the way he speaks in exclamations.

Here again, the answer is clearly in two parts and contains quotes and explanation.

Key Prose Terms

KEY TERMS

Make sure you understand and use these terms when answering Close Reading questions on prose:

- **character**
- **action**
- **plot**
- **description**
- **dialogue**
- **theme**
- **setting**
- **language**
- **imagery.**

Look up pages 78–80 for a definition of each term.

Close Reading of Poetry

ACTION to TAKE

Read the poem below. How can you tell it is a poem?

Preludes

(i)

THE winter evening settles down
With smell of steaks in passageways.
Six o'clock.
The burnt-out ends of smoky days.
And now a gusty shower wraps
The grimy scraps
Of withered leaves about your feet
And newspapers from vacant lots;
The showers beat
On broken blinds and chimney-pots,
And at the corner of the street
A lonely cab-horse steams and stamps.
And then the lighting of the lamps.

T.S. Eliot

Aspects of Poetry

You can tell this is a poem because it has these aspects:

- it is written in **verse**
- it **rhymes**
- it uses **imagery**
- it has lines of different lengths which creates **rhythm**
- it creates a **mood** through the special **language** used.

ACTION to TAKE

Read the poem again and pick out examples of each of these aspects.

Now look at the questions on the poem. Can you tell what each question is asking you to do?

Try to answer each question before looking at the model answer.

Questions with model answers

1. What is the poet describing?

The poet is describing a depressing urban scene.

2. Quote two words which give an impression of emptiness.

'Burnt-out' and 'vacant' give an impression of emptiness.

3. Does the poet have a positive or negative attitude to the scene he describes? Quote a word or phrase as evidence for your answer.

I feel the poet is negative about the scene. He concentrates on depressing images of decay, for example, 'lonely cab-horse' and 'broken blinds'.

4. What feeling is created by the phrase

'The grimy scraps
Of withered leaves …'?

The feeling is of a town which is dying.

5. Why has the poet chosen to place '**Six o'clock.**' in a line on its own?

The poet has chosen to place these words in a line on their own to emphasise that the poem is set at the beginning of the evening, the start of darkness descending into night. It says time is running out and so adds to the negative and eerie atmosphere.

Key Poetry Terms

KEY TERMS

Make sure you understand and use these terms when answering Close Reading questions on poetry:

- **verse**
- **rhyme**
- **imagery**
- **rhythm**
- **mood**
- **language.**

Look up pages 78–80 for a definition of each term.

Close Reading of Drama

Remember

Plays are meant to be performed on the stage, so when you are reading a part of a play:

- **try to think of it being acted out**
- **put plenty of feeling into reading a part. This will help you to understand why a character behaves in a certain way.**
- **visit a theatre to see the play being performed if you can, or watch the film version.**

In drama, there is far less description to read than in a novel or short story. Because of this, the writer has to create mood through what the characters say and do. The questions on this extract ask you to analyse the characters' feelings from what they say.

ACTION to TAKE

Read this extract critically and then answer the questions.

Enter MACBETH

LADY MACBETH My husband?

MACBETH I have done the deed. Didst thou not hear a noise?

LADY MACBETH I heard the owl scream and the crickets cry.
Did not you speak?

MACBETH When?

LADY MACBETH Now.

MACBETH As I descended?

LADY MACBETH Ay.

MACBETH Hark, who lies i' th'second chamber?

LADY MACBETH Donaldbain.

MACBETH This is a sorry sight.
Looking on his hands

LADY MACBETH A foolish thought, to say a sorry sight.

MACBETH There's one did laugh in's sleep, and one cried, 'Murder!',
That they did wake each other; I stood, and heard them,
But they did say their prayers and addressed them
Again to sleep.

LADY MACBETH	There are two lodged together.
MACBETH	One cried 'God bless us!' and 'Amen' the other, As they had seen me with these hangman's hands. List'ning their fear, I could not say 'Amen' When they did say 'God bless us,'
LADY MACBETH	Consider it not so deeply.
MACBETH	But wherefore could not I pronounce 'Amen'? I had most need of blessing and 'Amen' Stuck in my throat.
LADY MACBETH	These deeds must not be thought After these ways; so, it will make us mad.
MACBETH	Methought I heard a voice cry, 'Sleep no more: Macbeth does murder sleep', the innocent sleep, Sleep that knits up the ravelled sleeve of care, The death of each day's life, sore labour's bath, Balm of hurt minds, great nature's second course, Chief nourisher in life's feast.
LADY MACBETH	What do you mean?
MACBETH	Still it cried, 'Sleep no more!' to all the house; 'Glamis hath murdered sleep', and therefore Cawdor Shall sleep no more: Macbeth shall sleep no more.
LADY MACBETH	Who was it, that thus cried? Why, worthy thane, You do unbend your noble strength to think So brainsickly of things. Go get some water And wash this filthy witness from your hand. Why did you bring these daggers from the place? They must lie there. Go carry them and smear The sleepy grooms with blood.
MACBETH	I'll go no more. I am afraid to think what I have done; Look on't again, I dare not.
LADY MACBETH	Infirm of purpose! Give me the daggers. The sleeping and the dead Are but as pictures; 'tis the eye of childhood That fears a painted devil. If he do bleed, I'll gild the faces of the grooms withal, For it must seem their guilt.

Exit.

from *Macbeth* by William Shakespeare

Questions

1. Look at lines 1–10 of the extract. Macbeth has just murdered King Duncan. How do Macbeth and Lady Macbeth react to this deed? Are they
   - hysterical?
   - nervous?
   - proud?
   - relieved?

   You may use one or more of these words in your answer.
2. How does Lady Macbeth react to Macbeth's statement '**This is a sorry sight.**'?
3. What does Lady Macbeth say to reassure Macbeth?
4. At what point does Lady Macbeth lose patience with Macbeth?
5. What does Lady Macbeth say she will do with the daggers?
6. Think about Macbeth and Lady Macbeth. Which character is the braver of the two? Give reasons for your answer.

Check it

Check your answers on page 40.

Key Drama Terms

KEY TERMS

Make sure you understand and use these terms when answering Close Reading questions on drama:

- **character**
- **setting**
- **theme**
- **plot**
- **structure**
- **stage directions**
- **language.**

Look up pages 78–80 for a definition of each term.

Close Reading of Media

During your course, you may watch an extract from a film or TV programme. You should watch and listen to it and then answer the questions using evidence and explanation.

As mentioned on page 11, you will not gain many marks for simply 'telling the story' of what happens in the film or programme. You will gain marks by showing you have understood the extract and can evaluate its impact using the correct terms.

Aspects of Media

- You should identify the film's **genre**: for example, is it a Western, a romantic comedy or a documentary?
- You might be asked about the **narrative** (the story or plot).
- You could comment on **representation** – everything about a character from what he/she wears to what he/she thinks.

- You might be asked to look at **lighting**, **sound** or **cinematography**.
- You might be asked about the ***mise en scène*** of a particular shot. You might be asked to comment on this in detail. This means you would discuss everything in the shot, including the actors, their costumes, the lighting and sound, the props and the colour.
- You could be asked about the **editing** or the work of the **director**.

Key Media Terms

KEY TERMS

Make sure you understand and use these terms when answering Close Reading questions on media:

- **genre**
- **lighting**
- ***mise en scène***
- **narrative**
- **sound**
- **editing**
- **representation**
- **cinematography**
- **direction.**

Look up pages 78–80 for a definition of each term.

CLOSE READING OF NON-FICTION

This section will help you tackle Close Reading of non-fiction passages in class as well as in the exam.

Close Reading of non-fiction is also called comprehension or interpretation – you read a passage and then answer questions about it.

Before you Read Critically

You can make Close Reading of non-fiction easier than it sounds. One way is to work out a lot of information about the passage before you start reading it in detail and before you read the questions. This will help you to understand the passage and to answer the questions later.

KEY SKILLS

Try to answer these four questions before you read a passage critically:

- **Is the passage non-fiction?**
- **What is its genre?**
- **Who is its audience?**
- **What is its purpose?**

Is the passage non-fiction?

What are the clues to look for?

- Check the **title** – is it the headline of a newspaper article, for instance?
- Check the **layout**. Remember that layout refers to what the writing looks like on the page. Layout has nothing to do with content.
  - Pictures and diagrams often accompany non-fiction texts.
  - Newspapers have a clear format of columns and photos.
  - Letters have a set layout (e.g. an address at the top).
  - If the passage is written in lines, verses, has rhyming words and a title, it is probably a poem!
- Check the **content** – what is the text about? If it includes facts, arguments for and against, opinions or evidence, it is likely to be non-fiction. If the content is imaginary, if it contains characters and imagery, or if it is set in a particular place or time, then it is likely to be fiction.

What is its genre?

Genre means type of text. When was the last time you went to the school or local library? You may have looked at romance books, thrillers, cookbooks, horror stories, Westerns and autobiographies. These are all different genres. The 'clues' which help you identify the genre of a piece of writing are called 'markers'.

Think about **how** you can identify the genre. For example, if you are looking at a newspaper article, it will have numerous 'markers'. It will contain any or all of the following:

- a headline
- subheadings
- pictures/photographs
- captions
- columns
- special vocabulary (e.g. 'witness', 'statement', 'parliament')
- the journalist's name.

Remember

Use a highlighter when you are looking at the passage – this way, you can highlight any 'markers' as you notice them.

Who is its audience?

Identify for whom the passage is written – the **audience**. For example, a leaflet about computers could be written for children without any knowledge of computing, or it might be written for computer experts! The language and content of the leaflet has to change depending on who is going to read it.

What is its purpose?

Identify the **purpose** of the passage – the reason it has been written. An advert is written to persuade people to buy a product; a set of instructions is written to give information. If you can work out the purpose, the questions will be much easier to answer.

Always remember that someone wrote the passage. This may be obvious but it helps you realise that the writer has a **point of view**. He/she is trying hard to give you a certain message. The writer may state his/her opinions directly, for example:

> I have always thought that the Scots do not deserve a Parliament of their own.

The writer may put over his/her point of view in a less direct way, for example:

> The time Gavin spent at school involved him in hours of work, early starts, late finishes, overtime (the teachers even called it 'homework')... and all of it unpaid!

The formal term for a writer's point of view is '**authorial stance**'. This phrase may not be used in the questions but you still may be asked to identify the writer's point of view.

ACTION to TAKE

Study the Credit level passage below.

- **Is it non-fiction?**
- **What genre is it?**
- **Who might read it? (i.e. Who is the audience?)**
- **Is it giving information, explaining or entertaining? (i.e. What is its purpose?)**

> The road ahead tapered to infinity, in stages. Hill led to hill led to hill, and at each summit the road abruptly shrank to half its width, then half its width again, until it became a hairline crack in the land, then a faint wobble in the haze, then nothing. From out of the nothing now came a speck. It disappeared. It resurfaced as a smudge, then as a fist-sized cloud. A while passed. Finally, on the nearest of the hilltops, a full-scale dust-storm burst into view. The storm enveloped a low-slung pick-up truck, which slowed and came to a standstill beside the car, open window to open window.
>
> "Run out of gas?"
>
> "No"—I waved the remains of a hideous sandwich. "Just having lunch."

Did you work out that this is a piece of travel writing? It was written by Jonathan Raban, a very famous travel writer. He is describing his experiences in Montana in America.

This could also be a piece of fiction – in other words, a made-up piece of travel writing. We have no way of knowing since travel writing has a lot in common with fiction writing – for example, both genres use description and they might both be written in the first person ('I', 'my', 'we').

Reading Critically

Now you are ready to read the passage. A good idea is to skim the text quickly to get a general idea of what it is about. **Skimming** means you do not have to understand everything in detail. **First, just read through quickly…**

Now read the text again. **This second time, read every word carefully**. Do not worry if there are parts you do not understand. Read them over but then move on. You may find that the questions will help you work out the meaning.

When you read non-fiction critically, ask yourself these questions:

- **Is the language formal or informal?**
- **What style has the writer used?**
- **Is it fact or opinion?**

Is the language formal or informal?

Even if you have only skimmed through a text, you should be able to say what kind of language has been used. Firstly, is it formal or informal? Look at the lists below:

Formal language	*Informal language*
has no abbreviations uses long, complex sentences contains complex words	uses abbreviations uses short, simple sentences uses simple, everyday words

Now look at the two sentences below. Which is formal?

Robert agitated his head and declaimed, 'I am not to blame. It was not me.'

Bob shook his head and said, 'It wisnae me. I didnae dae it.'

Were you right? The first is formal because it contains complex words and no abbreviations. The second is informal because it contains abbreviations, simple vocabulary and colloquial phrases.

What style has the writer used?

Is it direct and straightforward or is it full of imagery? A writer is using imagery if he/she uses similes, metaphors or personification.

Again, look at the two sentences below. Which is direct and which uses imagery?

> The steel oil rig supports the drill.

> The mechanical monster embraces the corkscrew-like drill.

Were you right? The first is direct. The second contains a **metaphor** (describing the oil rig as a monster), **personification** (the oil rig is described as 'embracing' the drill as if it could carry out human actions) and a **simile** (the drill is described as a corkscrew).

Is it fact or opinion?

While you are skimming through a non-fiction passage, you will find clues which help you work out whether the passage is **fact** or **opinion**. For example, in an advertisement

- you may read facts:

> Marvellous Marvelon actually reduces cholesterol by 29%.

- you may also read opinions:

> Marvellous Marvelon tastes better than any other low-fat spread.

Facts are **statements** which are true and which cannot be argued about.

Opinions are **beliefs** that some people hold. They often start with 'I feel …' and 'It is my belief …' Opinions are more difficult to spot without these phrases, but all you have to do is ask yourself 'Is this a fact which cannot be questioned?' If the answer is no, you are reading an opinion!

ACTION to TAKE

Now study this General level passage below. Is it written in formal or informal language? What style does the writer use? Is the passage fact or opinion?

> When I moved to a flat in New York and discovered that my new neighbours included a colony of pigeons, my first reaction was: exterminate the brutes! I cringed at their morning mating calls, and agreed with my wife, Dana, when she cursed them as winged rodents that soil the city. I attacked them with broom and water-pistol. It was hard for me to believe that the traditional symbol of peace, a dove with an olive branch, is actually a white pigeon.

Did you work out that the language in this passage is **informal**? (You can tell because of the use of slang, e.g. 'brutes', and the exclamation mark.) The author moving to New York, finding a colony of pigeons and attacking them are facts. The **style** he is using is conversational and humorous. His **opinion** is that these birds are brutes and should be exterminated! The passage is from a newspaper article by John Tierney.

Answering the Questions

DOs and DON'Ts

Once you have read the passage critically:

✗ don't immediately start answering each question one by one.

✔ do read through all of the questions first, to find out:

- **how many there are**
- **what kind of questions they are**
- **which questions you find difficult and which you find easy.**

This will help you to manage your time more effectively.

The questions about a non-fiction passage may ask you to find out:

- **What is the writer's main message?**
- **How does the writer convey his/her ideas?**
- **What is the writer's point of view?**
- **What techniques has the writer used?**

What is the writer's main message?

The writer of a text usually has one main message that he/she is trying to get across. **The title may help you.** Read the passage carefully, looking for the main ideas.

Remember

As you read the passage, use a highlighter to highlight any words or phrases which you think might be important.

It is also a good idea to highlight key words in the questions.

In a non-fiction text, the writer often puts forward his/her main message in the first few paragraphs (and sometimes repeats it in the conclusion).

When you are explaining the main message in a text, **use your own words**. Of course, you can use quotations as evidence but you must explain in your own words why you have used the quote. By doing this, you show that you understand the message.

How does the writer convey his/her ideas?

A writer can convey his/her ideas in very subtle ways. These kinds of ideas are more difficult to find because they are 'hidden'. You have to look behind the straightforward meaning of the words to find the writer's message. For example:

- if a writer describes a sunrise, characters getting up and the sound of a postman at the door, we can work out that it is morning without the writer actually saying so.

The meaning behind any word(s) is called the '**connotation**'. A connotation is the association we make in our minds when we read or hear a word or words. For example:

- you know that the word 'football' refers to a game played by two teams which lasts 90 minutes. You will also have connotations for this word: if you love going to football games, the word will have pleasant associations (e.g. players, exciting, pies); if you hate football, the word will have negative connotations for you (e.g. boring, violent, fans, cold).

Writers choose words deliberately for their connotations. For example:

- if an author is against blood sports, he/she will describe them as 'bloodthirsty', 'cruel' or 'barbaric' to persuade you to agree with his/her point of view. This is what we mean when we say that there are hidden meanings in words.

Using words with particular connotations is only one way a writer can try to persuade the reader. There are other techniques such as **repetition** (repeating words or phrases) and **emphasis** (making a word or phrase more important than other words, e.g. by underlining or placing a word in an important position) which can help a writer make a point.

In a non-fiction piece, the writer will also find **evidence** to back up his/her arguments. This evidence could be in the form of statistics, statements from experts or real-life examples.

What is the writer's point of view?

Whatever the topic, a writer always has a point of view to put across. If the passage you are reading is about vegetarianism, then the writer will have a point of view either for or against this topic. The writer may state directly what he/she feels or give examples which make this clear. You will have to comment on how the writer puts across these views. You also have to justify (give reasons for) your comments from your own personal experience or knowledge as well as quoting from the passage itself.

What techniques has the writer used?

Writers have various techniques which they use to write effectively. These include their use of: register, genre, language, structure and figures of speech.

Key Non-fiction Terms

KEY TERMS

Make sure you understand and use these terms when answering Close Reading questions on non-fiction:

- **register**
- **genre**
- **language**
- **structure**
- **figures of speech.**

Look up pages 78–80 for a definition of each term.

CLOSE READING EXAM SKILLS

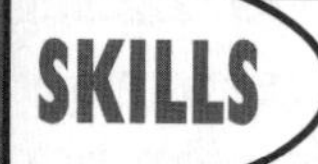

In your Reading exam, it is important that you:

- **know the format**
- **read the introduction and study any photographs**
- **read the questions carefully and identify key words**
- **write your answers in the answer booklet**
- **check how much to write**
- **quote if requested**
- **have a go at every question**
- **don't spend too long on any one question**
- **make your meaning clear**
- **check for bold type in the questions**
- **know what the questions are asking you to do.**

Know the format

Each Reading exam paper you sit will have the same format: there will be a passage (it can be fiction or non-fiction) followed by questions.

- The Foundation passage is usually short and will be clearly presented. It will be about things which are familiar to you.
- The General passage may be on a topic which is not so familiar to you and may be slightly longer.
- The Credit passage may contain unfamiliar complex ideas and may be quite long.

Read the introduction and study any photographs

There is always an introduction to the passage. There might also be a photograph with a caption to accompany a newspaper article. Many students do not bother to read the introduction or study the photograph but you should look at them very carefully – they are there to help you and can give you a good idea of what the passage is about and may even help you to work out something you don't understand in the passage itself.

For example, read this introduction to a previous Credit Reading exam passage:

> **In this extract the writer gives his impression of an area of Montana called the Badlands.**

Even before you start reading, you know that you are only going to read part of a text, that the writer is a man, that he is giving his opinions and that the Badlands is the name of an area in America.

Read the questions carefully and identify key words

Read over each question at least twice so you are sure what you are being asked. Many pupils read the questions too quickly and get the answer wrong. Be certain about what you are being asked to find. You will find this easier if you use a highlighter (or simply underline) to highlight any key words in the question. This will help you to focus on what you are being asked. For example, in the question

> **Quote two expressions from this section that continue the comparison between the prairie and the ocean.**

you might highlight '**two**', '**comparison**', '**prairie**' and '**ocean**'.

Write your answers in the answer booklet

In the exam, you should write your answers in the answer booklet provided.

Check how much to write

The amount of space that you are given after a question gives a good idea of how much you should write. In fact, some questions may be multiple choice or may only require a one-word answer. Check how much the question is worth – the number of marks on offer is also a good indication of how much to write.

Quote if requested

For each question, you will be told if you should quote from the passage or if you should answer in your own words. Remember that:

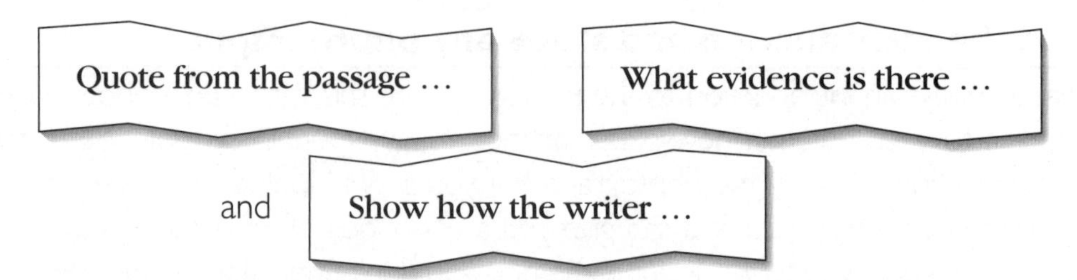

all require you to quote **actual words** and **phrases** from the text.

Have a go at every question

You may just be right! If you are unsure about a question, leave that question and go back to it when you have finished the others. Looking at a question afresh can sometimes help.

Don't spend too long on any one question

Don't spend too long on any one question – under exam stress, you may check your watch to discover you have wasted ten minutes on a question worth one or two marks.

Make your meaning clear

If the marker can't understand your answer, you won't get any marks. This also applies to over-writing (or waffling). If the marker cannot find the answer, you won't get any marks.

Check for bold type in the questions

Any words printed in **bold type** are important, e.g.

> Write down two **separate** expressions that suggest the policemen were **not expecting** trouble.

In this question, your attention is being drawn to the fact that you have to find two different quotes and that you should look for words which mean '**not expecting**' (for example 'unprepared').

Know what the questions are asking you to do

KEY SKILLS

Close Reading questions on non-fiction will ask you to:
- **identify a link**
- **evaluate a writer's effectiveness**
- **identify the writer's or a character's attitude**
- **identify a specific writing feature**
- **find specific expressions**
- **give reasons for your answers.**

1. A question may ask you to **identify a link** in the passage, e.g.

> How does the writer establish the link between paragraph 4 and paragraph 5?

   To answer this type of question, look at the structure of the passage. Writers usually link paragraphs in two ways:
   - they use **linking words** including 'however', 'finally' or 'After that …'
   - they **link through their ideas**. (For example, the author might discuss the problems connected with global warming in one paragraph and solutions to the problems in the next paragraph.)

2. A question may ask you to **evaluate the writer's effectiveness**. This type of question is asking you **how well** the writer has done his/her job. First, you have to work out what the writer is trying to do. Perhaps he/she is trying to build up a tense atmosphere, perhaps trying to persuade you by repeating a point, perhaps describing a scene in great detail. The question:

> How effective do you find this?

   is asking **your opinion** on whether the writer has chosen the best phrase to create that tense atmosphere or whether you think the writer has succeeded in helping you picture a scene. It is not sufficient to answer 'yes' or 'no' – you must explain why it was or was not effective.

3. A question may ask you to **identify the writer's or a character's attitude**. A word of warning – be sure whose attitude you are being asked about. Look at the difference between

> What is the *author's attitude* to the police?

and **What does the author suggest about the *attitude of the police*?**

The first is asking about the attitude of the writer and the second is asking about the attitude of the police.

To find the answer to this type of question, look for descriptive words such as 'delighted', 'horrified', 'aggressive' or 'unusual'.

4. A question may ask you to **identify a specific writing feature**. A writing feature is a writing technique. Every author uses features – these add together to create a particular author's writing style. For instance, a writer may use very long sentences or words which sound harsh (words with consonants such as 't' and 'd') and may like to use similes. In a question such as

   Identify any one feature of the writing …

   you should pick out one of these features.

5. A question may ask you to **find specific expressions in the passage**, e.g.

   Quote the expression that emphasises the idea of prejudice.

   To answer this type of question, you should look for a phrase with the same meaning as, or stronger meaning than, 'prejudice' or 'bias'. If another question asks you to

   Explain what this expression adds …

   you are being asked why a writer has used a particular word or phrase. Remember that **an author chooses words very carefully** and uses them for a reason. Perhaps he/she is trying to build up an atmosphere or convey an attitude.

6. A question may ask you to **give reasons for your answer**. You will frequently be asked for your reasons for an answer, e.g.

   Give a reason for your answer.

   or **Justify your answer.** or **Why?**

   The question:

   What is surprising about the boy's reaction? Give a reason for your answer.

may be worth three marks. You may get one mark for answering:

> It is surprising that the boy is not nervous.

You might get the other two marks for giving the reason.

ACTION to TAKE

Read the passage below critically and then make up six questions about the passage. Your six questions must test each of the six KEY SKILLS on page 31. Use the examples on pages 31 to 33 to help you make up your own questions. The first one has been done for you.

1. How does the writer establish the link between paragraphs 2 and 3?
2.
3.
4.
5.
6.

It is a good idea to make up expected answers and a marking scheme as well.

Now ask a friend to answer your questions!

After breakfast on a bright, sunny morning, they paraded on the square, each group under its sergeant. Herded aboard trucks, the whole company was transported to Baldoon Aerodrome, where the men were to do their jumps. No one spoke much as they turned from the road and passed a sentry at the gate. Even the high-spirited Tam Devlin crouched down in a corner, with nothing to say for himself.

"We're first to jump," Sergeant Bolton informed his group. "Five men will go up with me in ten minutes' time. Hold yourself in readiness."

Alex could not still the tremor in his legs as he sat on the grass, waiting until the sergeant returned. His mouth felt like an oven that had long since overheated. Time and again, he looked up into the sky and asked himself why he had volunteered for the paratroops.

from *Dropping Zone* by P. Baillie

CRITICAL EVALUATIONS

Your folio includes three **Critical Evaluations** – in other words, three personal responses to literature you have read. Read these two words carefully – your writing has to be 'critical' and it has to be an 'evaluation'. Being critical doesn't automatically mean you have to be negative. It means that you are judging certain aspects of a text.

Making an evaluation means coming to a conclusion about how effective a writer has been and how worthwhile you think the text is overall.

Using the Correct Terms

KEY SKILL

It is vital that you use the correct terms when writing your Critical Evaluations. Refer to the Key Terms on pages 15, 17, 20, 21 and 28 for more information.

Having a Structure

KEY SKILLS

It is also vital that your Critical Evaluations are well structured. In each of your Critical Evaluations, make sure you:

- **include a title**
- **have an introduction**
- **have a main body**

- **analyse the text quoting evidence**
- **include personal opinions and reactions to aspects of the text**
- **write in the present tense**
- **have a conclusion.**

Include a title

Include a title for your work which gives a good indication of what your response is about. For example, the title *Macbeth* does not tell the marker very much! However, if you use the title *Ambition and how it destroys Macbeth*, the marker will be **very clear** about your topic. It will also help to keep you **focused** on the topic.

The title is important for another reason. In order to give you a grade for your response, the teacher or marker has to understand **your purpose**. This means you have to make clear what you are going to do and then do it! A marker grades you according to whether you have fulfilled your purpose – in this case, to explain how ambition destroys Macbeth. If you start writing about the witches and their supernatural habits halfway through, you cannot hope for a good grade, even if you make interesting points. The title you choose is **crucial** to your success.

It is helpful to highlight key words and phrases in a task. If a Critical Evaluation task asks

> **What techniques does Ted Hughes use in his poem *The Thought Fox* and how effective are they?**

you might highlight '**techniques**' and '**effective**'. Focus on these words when you are writing and you should fulfil the purpose of the task.

Have an introduction

Every Critical Evaluation must have an introductory paragraph. In this paragraph, you should set out the title of the text, the name of the author and, if appropriate, when the text was written and/or a quotation. The most crucial sentence, however, **states your purpose** – it explains what you are going to write about. If you choose the title *Ambition and how it destroys Macbeth*, your first paragraph might contain a sentence similar to

> I will write about why I think Macbeth is ambitious, what methods he uses to achieve his aims and how his ambition leads to his death.

Have a main body

Write the main body of your response in sections. For example, if you are writing the *Macbeth* response, three sections in the main body would be a good idea (you would use paragraphs within each of these sections):

- section 1 could consider reasons for his ambition
- section 2 could look at what he does to achieve power
- section 3 could discuss his death.

Analyse the text quoting evidence

To gain a Credit award, you must show that you are very familiar with the text. You will gain very few marks for simply 'telling the story'. You should analyse the ideas in the text. You could do this by referring to particular parts of it and by quoting evidence for the points you make.

Show that you have thought about the text and say what you have gained personally from it. Again, quote evidence for what you say. Use **critical terminology** (the correct terms) when discussing the text and quote or refer in detail to areas of the text.

Include personal opinions and reactions to aspects of the text

You should always include your own opinions and feelings about the text in your answer. If you laughed at the story, were angry at how the characters behaved or upset by a word in a poem, say so! Markers want to know that you have become involved in a text and have feelings about it. Remember that your feelings, reactions and opinions are not wrong – as long as you give good reasons and evidence for what you think.

Write in the present tense

Write about literature in the present tense. For example:

The author uses alliteration effectively.

and not 

The author used alliteration effectively.

Have a conclusion

Finish off your response by referring back to your original purpose or task. If you state in the title and the introduction that you are writing about *The importance of setting in the film 'The Great Gatsby'*, then the conclusion should include a paragraph giving your final opinion on this topic. For instance, you might write in your conclusion

All these examples of setting show the contrast between rich and poor which is one of the main themes of the film.

Choosing Critical Evaluations for your Folio

Your first two Critical Evaluations

Your first **two** Critical Evaluations for your folio must be responses to **two different genres** of literature: if your first is about a prose text (a novel, a short story, a biography or a piece of travel writing), then your second must be on a play or poem. If your first is on a poem, your second must be on a play or on prose.

Your third Critical Evaluation

Your third Critical Evaluation for your folio can be either

- **a response to a genre** you have written about already. For example, you may have written your first Critical Evaluation on a poem and your second on a play. Your third Critical Evaluation could be on a poem or a play as long as it is not the same poem or play you have already written about. It could also be on a different genre such as a novel or a short story.

or

- **a response to media** (a film, TV or radio programme). As mentioned on page 11, you comment on aspects of the media in detail in your response.

or

- **an imaginative response to a literary text**. This is a different type of response to a text. For example:
  - you may read a novel and then be asked to imagine you are a character from it
  - you may write a letter or a diary as if you were that character

- you may read a poem which is about a skating pond on a snowy day. Your teacher may ask you to imagine yourself being there and to write about an incident that might happen.

In each case, you should clearly use information from the text to give you ideas about what to write. You then just add your own imagination!

Examples of Critical Evaluations

A critical evaluation of a film

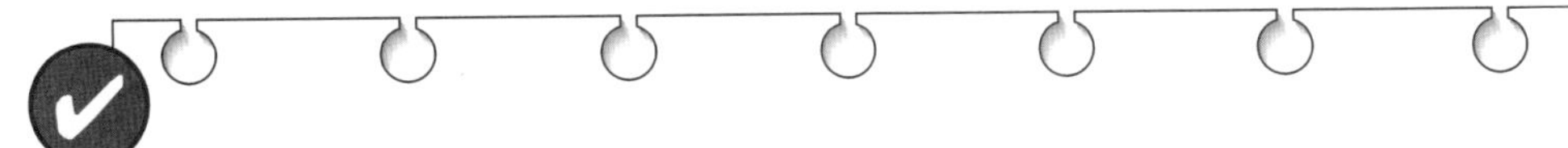

An evaluation of 'Dances with Wolves'

'Dances with Wolves' is a film directed by Kevin Costner. It is a Western but it is also a love story about the main character, John Dunbar, who falls in love with a white woman adopted by the Indians at birth. The film is really a mixture of two genres – a Western and a romance.

The main character, John Dunbar (acted by Costner) is represented as a 'hero'. For example, in the first 'mise en scène', he rides into battle expecting to die but he survives. The lighting in this scene, together with the restless music ...

A critical evaluation of a poem

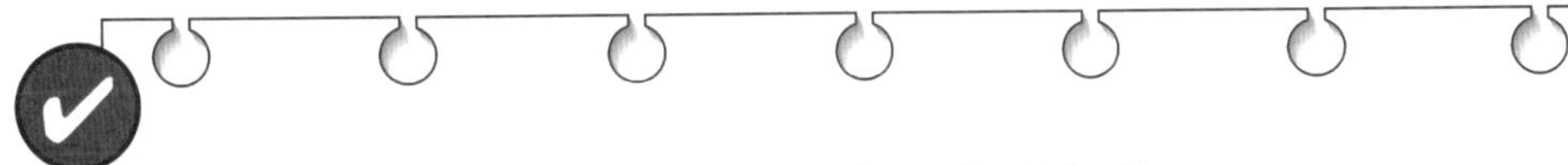

How characters are described in the poems
'The Adoption Papers' by Jackie Kay

'The Adoption Papers' by Jackie Kay is a series of poems about a coloured girl who was adopted in the 1960s. The poems are about how the girl reacts to her adoption. In certain parts the girl is speaking, but in others the adopting mother and the real mother are speaking. For example, 'Ma mammy says she's no really ma mammy' is the girl speaking.

The girl is confused about her adoption. In the first poem, where the girl is told she has been adopted ...

An imaginative response to a literary text

KEY SKILLS

In an imaginative response to a literary text, you should:

- **show you are very familiar with the text**
- **refer to relevant parts of the text**
- **try to create a mood, tone and style**
- **use writing techniques**
- **organise your writing appropriately.**

In this example, the student has read *Dulce et Decorum Est* (on page 39). It is a poem by Wilfred Owen which was written during the First World War. The student has then written an imaginative response as if he were in the trenches at the time. He has chosen to do this in the form of a letter home. He uses details and ideas from the poem in his story.

ACTION to TAKE

Study the student's letter below and see if you can pick out which ideas have come from the poem and which ideas the student has made up himself.

My Dear Jean

I am writing to you on our first rest day for over a fortnight. It has taken us two weeks to travel only a few miles.

We were marching towards our billet here in Pyres when we came under gas attack. It was the most terrible time, Jean. So many of the men were worn out and ill, bent over and barefoot. Then gas shells started to drop. They land so quietly, Jean, that many of the men did not hear them because they were already so tired and ready to fall.

The gas attack lasted only a few ...

Wilfred Owen
(1893-1918)

Dulce et Decorum Est

Bent double, like old beggars under sacks,
Knock-kneed, coughing like hags, we cursed through sludge,
Till on the haunting flares we turned our backs
And towards our distant rest began to trudge.
Men marched asleep. Many had lost their boots
But limped on, blood-shod. All went lame; all blind;
Drunk with fatigue; deaf even to the hoots
Of gas shells dropping softly behind.

Gas! GAS! Quick, boys! – An ecstasy of fumbling,
Fitting the clumsy helmets just in time;
But someone still was yelling out and stumbling,
And flound'ring like a man in fire or lime...
Dim, through the misty panes and thick green light,
As under a green sea, I saw him drowning.

In all my dreams, before my helpless sight,
He plunges at me, guttering, choking, drowning.

If in some smothering dreams, you too could pace
Behind the wagon that we flung him in,
And watch the white eyes writhing in his face,
His hanging face, like a devil's sick of sin;
If you could hear, at every jolt, the blood
Come gargling from the froth-corrupted lungs,
Obscene as cancer, bitter as the cud
Of vile, incurable sores on innocent tongues, –
My friend, you would not tell with such high zest
To children ardent for some desperate glory,
The old Lie: Dulce et decorum est
Pro patria mori.

France 1917

THE MOST IMPORTANT READING SKILL

This chapter has given you some advice about reading – Close Reading of fiction and non-fiction as well as advice on writing Critical Evaluations.

KEY SKILL

The most important reading skill to develop is the skill of reading critically – whether you are looking at a poem or at a poster in a shop window. By doing this, Standard Grade English will suddenly become a lot easier!

CRITICAL EVALUATION CHECKLIST

Use this checklist to assess each Critical Evaluation you write at school and at home. Fill in the boxes against each question. Use a tick or a cross to show what you have or have not done. Alternatively, ask your teacher or a friend to complete the boxes.

	Excellent	Good	OK	Try harder next time!
Are you thoroughly familiar with the text?	☐	☐	☐	☐
Have you analysed the main ideas?	☐	☐	☐	☐
Have you referred to parts of the text in detail?	☐	☐	☐	☐
Have you related these parts of the text to your title?	☐	☐	☐	☐
Have you explained what you have gained from the text?	☐	☐	☐	☐
Have you made a genuine personal response to the text using evidence?	☐	☐	☐	☐
Have you analysed the writer's techniques?	☐	☐	☐	☐
Have you used critical terminology?	☐	☐	☐	☐
Have you used quotations?	☐	☐	☐	☐
Have you organised your Critical Evaluation?	☐	☐	☐	☐
Have you selected the most important points and highlighted them?	☐	☐	☐	☐
Is your Critical Evaluation the correct length?	☐	☐	☐	☐

Model Answers to Macbeth questions on page 20

1. Macbeth and Lady Macbeth are hysterical and nervous. They speak in short breathless phrases and imagine they hear things.
2. Lady Macbeth tells Macbeth he is 'foolish' for saying 'This is a sorry sight.' She feels he is being stupid and should stop thinking about what he has done.
3. Lady Macbeth tells him not to think about what he has done – otherwise they will go mad.
4. When Lady Macbeth says 'Infirm of purpose!', she has lost patience with Macbeth because he is not making any sense.
5. She intends to smear blood on the grooms' faces so that it will look as though they carried out the murder.
6. I think Lady Macbeth is braver because Macbeth is nervous and scared – he says 'I am afraid to think what I have done.'

WRITING

Four Types of Writing

Key Writing Skills

1. Writing to Convey Information
2. Discursive Writing
3. Personal Experience Writing
4. Imaginative Writing

Writing for your Folio

Writing in the Exam

Writing Checklist

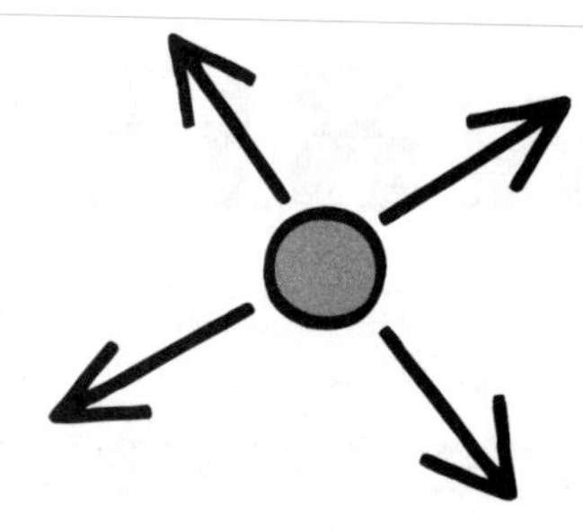

FOUR TYPES OF WRITING

During your Standard Grade course, you will develop your skills in **four** different types of Writing – two are transactional, two are expressive:

These two types are called **transactional**.

1. **writing to convey information** on a topic
2. **discursive writing** (writing in which you argue and evaluate a case)

These two types are called **expressive**.

3. **personal experience writing** (writing in which you describe a personal experience, or express your feelings and reactions to a topic)
4. **imaginative writing** in a specific literary form.

Before studying each of these types separately, let's first consider the key skills you need for all these types of writing.

KEY WRITING SKILLS

KEY SKILLS

For every piece of writing you do, make sure you:

- **have a plan**
- **know your audience and your purpose**
- **use correct spelling, punctuation and grammar**
- **don't be too long (or too short).**

Have a plan

Careful planning is essential before you start any piece of writing. Students often miss out this step which is a big mistake! The more careful your planning, the more effective your writing will be.

Imagine you are writing a story with the title *The Rhythm of Life*. Think about this title. What about creating a **mind map** with all your ideas? (This is similar to 'brainstorming'.)

First, turn your piece of paper sideways and draw a picture in the middle of the page. Perhaps this title gives you the idea of a drum… so draw a drum! Now draw lines coming out of the drum and write your ideas on each line. Now draw smaller lines coming out of the bigger lines and write even more ideas on these lines. Study the good example below.

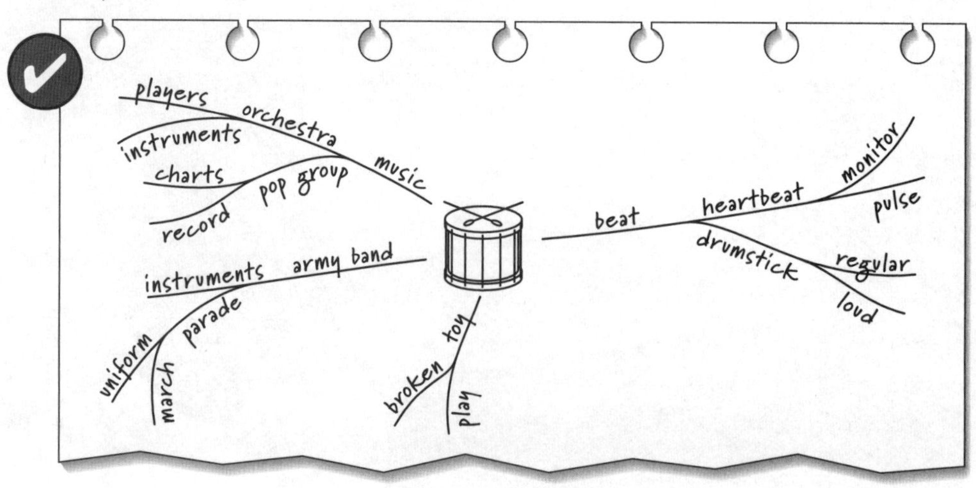

Now read the map carefully. What ideas do you like which could be used for the basis of a story? You could write a story about a premature baby with a heart defect or perhaps a story about a drummer in a band who achieves stardom and personal happiness.

You now have a basic idea for your story. Now start to think about the main **character(s)**:

- Who are they?
- What do they look like?
- How do they behave?
- What kind of people are they?
- How do they speak to/treat others?

Also start to think about the **shape** of your story:

- When will the climax (the most important/exciting part of the story) happen?
- What will happen at the end of your story?

If you are arguing and evaluating a case, planning is just as important. You will have a lot of your own ideas ready. You may have done a lot of research. You could draw a mind map similar to the one on page 42.

You must then **organise all your ideas into a sensible order**. Otherwise, your writing will be confused and confusing.

Think about and plan what you are going to write before you start. This will help you to make your piece of writing the right length and help to ensure that it is well organised and sticks to the topic. Planning is well worthwhile!

Know your audience and your purpose

Every piece of writing has an **audience** (the person/people who read(s) it) and a **purpose** (the reason for the piece being written).

- If you keep a diary, the audience is you (and only you if it is a secret diary). What is the purpose of a diary? Actually, a diary may have a number of purposes – to keep a record, to give information, to entertain or to reflect.
- If you are writing a story to be read by a small child, you should use a suitable style. You would use words a child would understand – simple, clear sentences and phrases which sound interesting. You might also use specific techniques, such as alliteration, to keep the child's attention while listening.
- If the purpose of a story is to entertain the reader, you must do things that will keep the reader interested. For example, you could use an effective opening which will make the reader want to keep reading. You could use good description which helps the reader form a picture in his/her mind. You could build up tension so the reader wants to continue reading.

Use correct spelling, punctuation and grammar

While you are writing, try to keep mistakes to a minimum! Remember the basic rules about capital letters, full stops, etc. Check over your writing for spelling mistakes after you have finished.

Try to make your meaning clear. The marker must be able to make sense of what you have written. He/she will also expect you to write in correct sentences and paragraphs.

Don't be too long (or too short)

The length of the writing should be 'appropriate to the purpose'. Try not to write too much – or too little!

For example:

- you would expect a poem to be shorter than a discursive essay about global warming
- in a piece of personal experience writing, you express your feelings and reactions. You spend some time describing these feelings and thoughts. You would be unlikely to be able to do this in only two or three paragraphs!

Let's now consider the **four** different types of writing in detail.

1. WRITING TO CONVEY INFORMATION

Examples of writing to convey information include writing about:

- how a volcano erupts
- your favourite pastime
- how to play a game (e.g. American Football)
- a scientific experiment
- an historical event
- your home-town
- another country
- your chosen career
- how a computer works.

When writing to convey information:

- **be selective about the information you include**
- **put the information in order**
- **make your essay interesting.**

Be selective about the information you include

When writing to convey information, you should include a lot of **information** (facts about the topic). However, the best essays of this type do not just list a number of facts in a random order. Instead, they are selective – they don't include all the facts you have found or know, only those which are the most interesting or important.

Put the information in order

You then put these ideas in a good order. You could put the most important facts first or later – it's up to you. If a writer was writing about her home-town of Dunfermline, she would mention its location, age, size and facilities but might save information about the Abbey and Pittencrieff Park until the end because she considers these to be the most attractive features of the town. Alternatively, she might highlight them at the very beginning. It's up to the writer!

Make your essay interesting

Have you ever heard the saying 'Knowledge is power'? In the case of writing to convey information, this is definitely true! The more knowledge you can display about the topic, the better. However, avoid simply cramming your essay full of dry facts. Make your essay interesting by using techniques such as expressing yourself with humour or choosing less well-known facts. It is important that you communicate your enthusiasm for the topic to your readers.

DON'T

✗ **Don't include any storytelling or extended description of feelings or personal reflections in an essay which conveys information.**

Here is an extract from an essay conveying information about a career in catering. Notice how it is packed with facts:

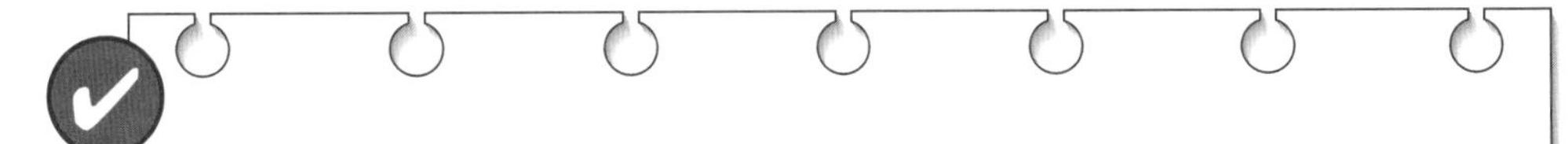

A CAREER IN CATERING

A career in catering usually begins with the person being interested in and enthusiastic about cooking of all types. Entry to a college at age eighteen depends more on showing interest in cooking than in having experience. Of course, experience helps and budding chefs should try to gain experience in kitchens, perhaps at weekends or in the evenings before they leave school. They must be prepared to 'muck in' and wash dishes as well as watch the chef at work.

College courses teach theory and practice. Theory includes understanding health regulations, safety in the kitchen, and involves reading catering books. Practice means actually reading and cooking recipes ...

2. DISCURSIVE WRITING

In discursive writing (also called 'argumentative writing'), you argue and evaluate a case.

Here are examples of topics for discursive writing:

- euthanasia
- the Royal Family
- hunting
- school uniform
- animal rights
- self-government
- vegetarianism
- football fans
- children's rights
- freedom of speech
- private schools
- racism.

Are there any that you feel strongly about?

KEY SKILLS

When writing a discursive essay you should:

- **choose a topic you feel strongly about**
- **be sure of your opinion before you start and be consistent**
- **include background information in your introduction**
- **argue using evidence**
- **evaluate the opposite argument**
- **use formal language**
- **give your essay a good structure.**

Choose a topic you feel strongly about

You probably have opinions on many different topics but is there one you have a real interest in? This would be a good one to choose.

Be sure of your opinion before you start and be consistent

It is essential to be sure about your opinion before you start writing. Never change your mind in the middle of your writing – you must be consistent in your argument!

Decide before you start:

- **are you for?**

  If you are for a topic, you should put forward ideas to support your opinion. Only mention ideas against the topic if you can refute (argue against) them. Otherwise you are undermining your own opinions.

- **are you against?**

  If you are against a topic, you should put forward ideas to support your opinion. Only mention ideas for the topic if you can refute them.

- **are you undecided?**
  If you are undecided, you should put forward both sides of the argument. You should try to balance your opinions.

Include background information in your introduction

For example, if you are writing about the monarchy, include details of what the monarchy is, where and how the monarchy operates in this country and perhaps some historical notes about royal families. This helps the reader have a clear understanding of the topic. However, keep this section of your essay brief.

It is very important that you clearly state your opinion in your introduction. Then the reader will be clear from the start about your point of view.

Argue using evidence

You then argue your case – you state your opinions and then produce supporting evidence for them. Your evidence might be statistics or other facts. You can use evidence from your reading or from interviews with other people. For example, if you are arguing in favour of the monarchy, you could have carried out research on how popular the Royal Family is both here and abroad and use the statistics in your essay. Your evidence might be in the form of quotes from people who support the monarchy. Think of as many reasons for keeping the monarchy as you can. If you include only one or two reasons, your essay will not be very convincing. It is important that your ideas are thought-provoking.

Check it

The main purpose of this type of writing is to persuade the reader that you are right in your views. Have you convinced your readers?

Evaluate the opposite argument

Try to evaluate the arguments of the other side. For example, if you are for the monarchy, you could write:

Many people consider the Royal Family to be an outdated institution. However, I feel that recent events have made the monarchy reflect and change its outlook. For example, Prince William is often shown in the media enjoying typical teenage activities.

When you are evaluating the argument of the other side, it is important that you remain objective – you 'stand back' from the topic and consider the merits of the opposite argument.

Use formal language

Notice the formal language used in the examples on page 47 and below – you must write discursive essays in a clear, formal **tone**.

Give your essay a good structure

Use paragraphs to organise your essay and to help make your arguments clear to the reader.

Remember to **include a conclusion** in a discursive essay. This is a finishing-off paragraph in which you **summarise** your views and restate your opinion. If you have been writing a balanced essay in which you explain both sides of the case, you must summarise both sides in your conclusion.

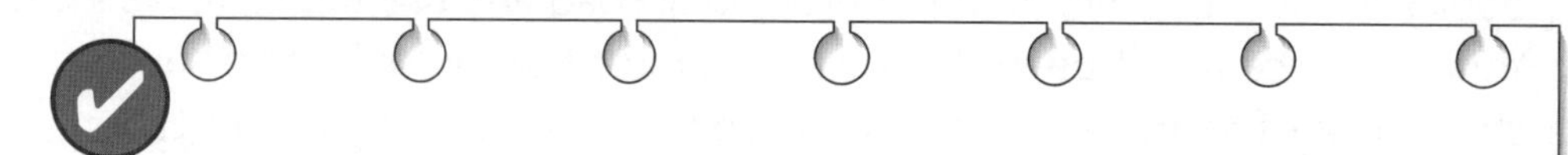

Study the start of the discursive essay below – notice how the writer gives her opinion and includes plenty of examples.

DRUGS IN SPORT

Recently, it has been alleged that Linford Christie took drugs to improve his performance. The famous American runner, 'Flo-Jo' Johnson, was also accused of taking drugs. These well-known athletes now have questions over their Olympic gold medals because of these accusations.

I think drug-taking is completely wrong for sportsmen and women for many reasons and especially because of the respect these athletes could lose.

Firstly, athletes should compete equally and it is unfair that some have an advantage because steroids have built up their muscles. For example, in the 1980 Olympics ...

There is a lot to consider when writing a discursive essay. You might find you are very good at this type – try it and see!

3. PERSONAL EXPERIENCE WRITING

In personal experience writing, also called 'personal reflective writing', you describe a personal experience, express your feelings about it and give your reactions to it. Many students think this is the easiest type of essay to write, but don't be fooled! You have to describe the experience you choose in great detail, as well as express your feelings about it in detail too. Your reflections after the event are also an important part of this type of essay.

KEY SKILLS

To write a good personal experience essay, make sure you:

- **don't invent the experience**
- **describe the experience in detail**
- **express your feelings about the experience**
- **reflect on the experience.**

Don't invent the experience

Never make up an experience! Markers are good at spotting the difference between someone who is describing a real event he/she has attended and someone who is making the whole thing up! If you have never been on a protest march, you will find it difficult to explain your feelings and reactions to it in a convincing way.

Describe the experience in detail

Tell the reader all about the experience:

- What happened?
- How did it start?
- Where did it take place?
- Who were you with?
- What was the atmosphere like?
- Did things go according to plan?
- How did it end?

Tell the reader what things looked like and what sounds you heard. Use your five senses to describe what you saw, touched, smelt, heard and tasted. Use lots of detail – the more detail you use, the more interesting your writing will be.

In this type of writing, the SQA is looking for you to show **insight**. Showing insight means that you have realised something, that you have really thought in depth about what the experience has meant to you. Writing a sentence like

> *I realised very early in our holiday that the beggars who appeared every day did not mean to annoy us – they were just trying to get a few pennies from rich tourists.*

shows insight.

Express your feelings about the experience

Tell the reader how you felt – before the event, during it and afterwards. Were you nervous, excited or scared? Were you proud, upset or angry?

Remember that your readers want to know how you felt. Don't forget to include your feelings and reactions **throughout** your writing – do not add them on at the end in one big section.

Reflect on the experience

This part usually comes at the end of your writing. You should look back on your experience and reflect on it (even if it was only a few days ago). You could explain how you learned something about yourself from the experience: perhaps you changed because of it; perhaps your feelings and reactions surprised you. Reflect on the event – drawing a mind map may help you.

The SQA is looking for you to show **self-awareness** in this type of writing – you must show that you are aware of your own feelings and reactions and understand why you behaved the way you did. For example, writing a sentence like

> I know now that I was behaving like a spoilt child, but at the time I felt so betrayed by my mum. After all, I was only eight!

shows real self-awareness.

Always try to explain your feelings – show the reader that you have reflected in depth and that you are aware of how and why you behaved as you did.

ACTION to TAKE

Compare the two examples below. Why is the second better?

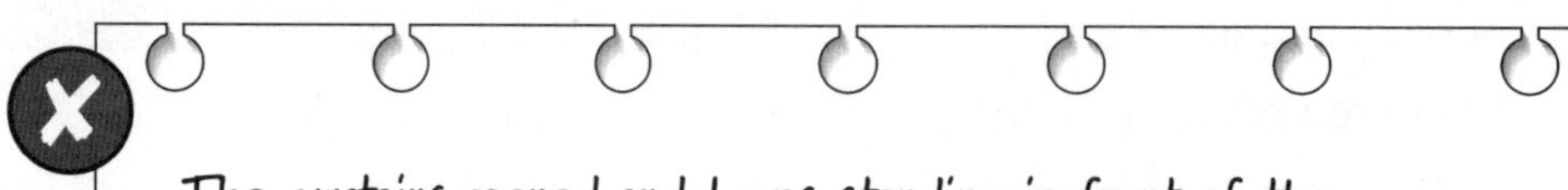

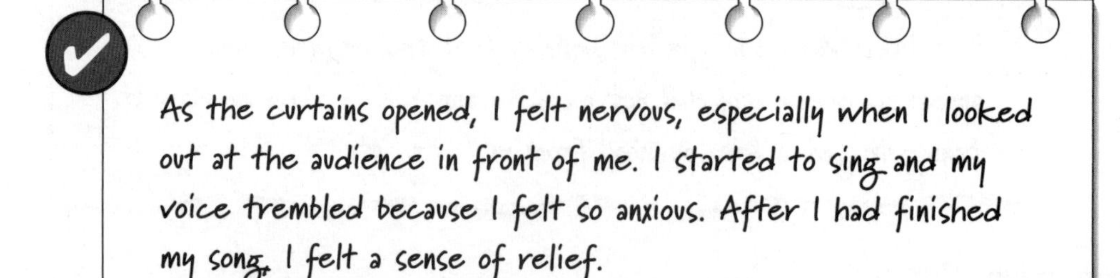

In this next example, the student is writing about an audition for a theatre company. Notice how well he describes his feelings, while also giving clear information about what he was doing:

MY AWFUL AUDITION

Last May, I auditioned for a place in the Caledonian Youth Theatre. This is a Scottish group which has actors from all over Scotland. They put on plays in the Edinburgh Festival Fringe and they have residential weekends and a summer school. I was desperate to join but first I had to overcome my nerves!

It took ages, but I decided to act out a scene from 'Romeo and Juliet'. This is my favourite play and I chose the speech from the balcony scene where ...

4. IMAGINATIVE WRITING

In imaginative writing you write imaginatively in a specific literary form. This type of writing may be in the form of a short story, a letter, a diary, a poem, a drama script or a biography.

You may enjoy writing imaginative stories or poems. You may be good at writing letters. Maybe you write a diary, so you might be good at writing an imaginary diary entry as though you were someone else. First decide whether you are good at imaginative writing: if you like reading stories or poems, this could be the type for you.

To develop your imaginative writing, make sure you:

- **read other writers and identify their styles**
- **use particular conventions for effect**
- **practise often.**

Read other writers and identify their styles

Reading examples of the different literary forms will help you a great deal with writing each form. The more you read, the more you will learn about how other writers develop ideas. The best way to understand the conventions of a particular form is to read plenty of examples of the form. This way you will become familiar with what is expected.

Use particular conventions for effect

You will be marked not only on the content of your chosen literary form – the ideas and words you use – but also on the conventions you use. The conventions of a genre are the aspects of a piece of writing that make it a specific literary form.

- The conventions of a **short story** are that it is brief, has characters, a setting and one main event.
- The conventions of a **poem** are that it is written in lines, uses rhyme and/or rhythm, and deals with a topic or theme.
- The conventions of a **drama** are that it has stage directions, has characters revealing their personalities through dialogue, moves in scenes and acts towards a climax.
- The conventions of a **letter** are that it is written in the first person, has a specific layout (that is to say, the address, date, salutation and ending must be correctly placed) and content.

ACTION to TAKE

Which particular literary form uses these conventions?

- **written in the first person ('I', 'my', 'we')**
- **can be written in the present tense**
- **includes reflections, feelings, thoughts, insights**
- **can be written in short phrases**

Did you work out this is a diary or journal?

Practise often

As with all types of writing, the more you practise writing imaginatively, the better you will become.

Let's now look at how to write imaginatively in two forms: a short story and a letter.

Writing a Short Story

To write a short story well, remember to:

- **use your imagination**
- **choose an interesting setting**
- **make an interesting start**
- **invent two or three main characters**
- **decide who will tell your story**
- **have a structure with one main event**
- **include description, dialogue and narrative**
- **make your ending match what has happened.**

Let's work through an example using the title *Stranded*.

Use your imagination

Consider the title *Stranded*. What is the first thing you think of? A desert island? Most people would probably think the same. So use your imagination to make your story a little bit **different** – what about being stranded in time, or at an airport?

What about the idea of two time travellers who are stranded in time and place? They could be brother and sister. The story could be for children so I might make the characters children, too. I must be careful to bear my audience in mind – the language must be easy for children to understand.

Use the mind map technique (or brainstorm in your own way) to explore the topic. Think about stories you have read that may give you ideas.

Check it

Check back to page 42 for information about mind maps.

Now the fun starts. It's time to make choices!

Choose an interesting setting

It is a good idea to make the setting for your story one with which you are familiar. Then you can describe it in great detail.

However, I have chosen an unfamiliar setting for my story so I will have to use my imagination…

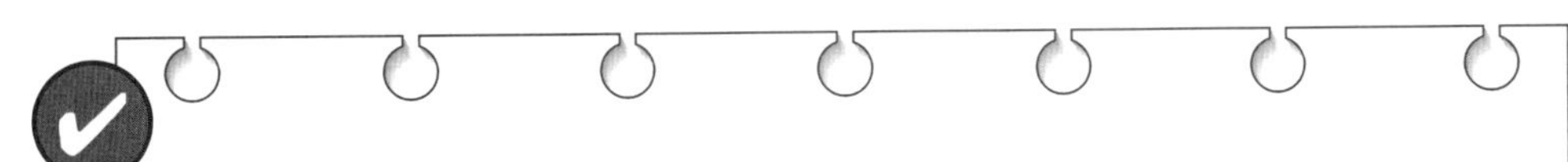

'We're lost!' shouted Tom, staring up into the whirlpool of smoke and wind. 'I don't know where we are and I don't know when we are, either!'

'Calm down, Tom, or we'll never get out of here!' Tilly shouted back.

The whirlpool slowly dissolved while they waited and the children found themselves standing on damp grey earth and feeling a cold chill down their backs. The place – wherever it was – was deserted. The time – whenever it was – was unknown. Tom and Tilly began to shiver.

Make an interesting start

Get the reader hooked! Create an interesting opening by using such techniques as dialogue, one single word, a description, a short phrase or a long complex sentence.

I started my *Stranded* story with:

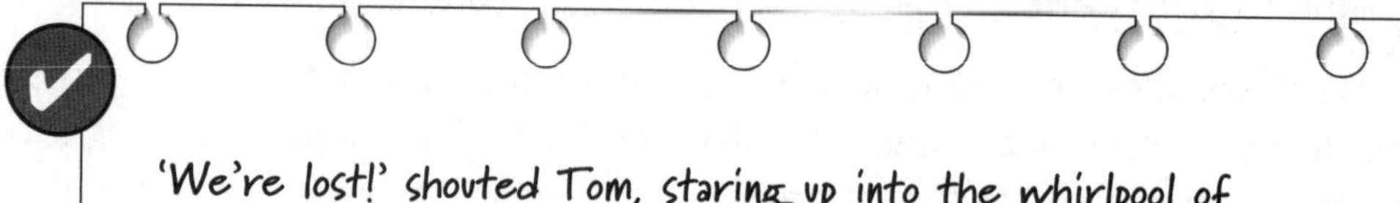

Invent two or three main characters

Invent two or three main characters, but no more. This helps keep your short story to an appropriate length.

Think about:

- what they look like
- how they behave
- what their personalities are
- how they treat others.

You can describe the characters directly:

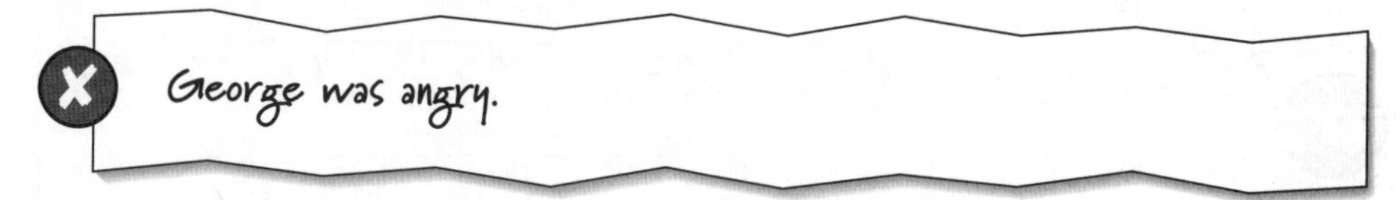

or show what they are like through how they behave:

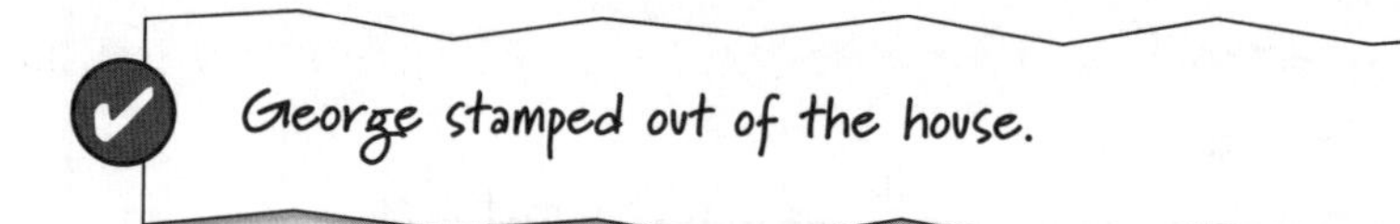

or through what they say in dialogue:

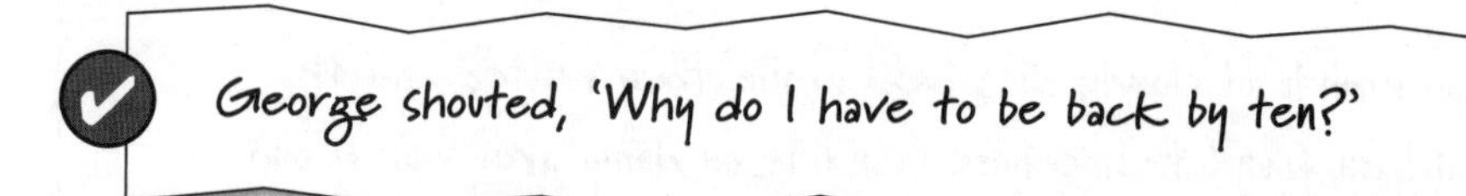

Do you agree that the second and third examples are more interesting than the first?

Decide who will tell your story

Will one of the characters tell the story (using the first person, 'I') or do you want to use the third person to describe the action (using 'he' or 'she')? For example, either

I swung back the heavy vines and immediately felt a cool breeze on my face.

or

He swung back the heavy vines and immediately felt a cool breeze on his face.

Choose the one which is the best for your story. For *Stranded*, I will use the third person.

Have a structure with one main event

Your plot must have a structure with one main event. Decide when the main event will happen. I think I would like the main event to happen quite late in my story so that I can build up to a climax.

Include description, dialogue and narrative

To make your story interesting, make sure you include:

- **description** (of characters, setting, atmosphere)
- **dialogue** (what characters say to others and to themselves)
- **narrative** (parts which 'tell the story').

ACTION to TAKE

Can you work out which example below is descriptive, which is dialogue and which is narrative?

1. Andrea whispered under her breath, 'What am I doing here?'

2. The heavy heat of the sun made the grasses wilt.

3. The boys broke open the garage doors and stole the van.

Answers: 1. dialogue 2. descriptive 3. narrative

So far in my story, I have concentrated on description and dialogue. Time for some narrative…

As the mist swirled round them, Tom and Tilly started to walk towards the horizon. They pulled their jackets closer around them and stepped carefully over the clay underneath with damp bare feet. 2000 and the stifling heat of Florida seemed a lifetime away.

Make your ending match what has happened

In a light story, full of fun and comedy, you would not expect a very sad ending with all the characters being killed!

Look at the ending of my story now. Do you think it matches the beginning?

'I don't know about you, Tilly, but I am certainly ready for a holiday. What about going back to where we started – Florida in 2000?'

The time machine stuttered as it started after its long rest. Slowly it lifted and began to spiral upwards …

ACTION to TAKE

If you have enjoyed the *Stranded* example, why not complete it by writing the main body of the story?

Writing a Letter

Much of the advice about short story writing applies to the letter. For example, you must have a structure and include description.

If you choose to write a letter, the conventions you use must be absolutely correct.

Check it

Look back to page 52 to check the conventions of a letter.

KEY SKILLS

To write a good letter, remember to:
- **identify your audience and know your purpose**
- **use the first person**
- **have a structure**
- **choose the appropriate language.**

You may be asked to write a personal letter or a business letter. Be sure which type you are being asked to write. The rest of the advice in this section is based on writing a personal letter.

Identify your audience and know your purpose

Your audience and purpose are crucial if you are writing a letter. Who are you writing to and why are you writing?

Use the first person

The **narrative voice** refers to which pronoun is used in a piece of writing. In a letter, the first person is used. For example,

I feel humiliated by what you did ...

or

I want to let you know that you behaved ...

Have a structure

The structure of your letter is up to you, depending on the content you have decided. For instance, you might write a letter as if you are a servant in Victorian times far away from home. In this case, a sensible structure might be to describe the house in which you are working and the family you are working for in the main body of the letter, and then your feelings and hopes at the end of the letter.

Choose the appropriate language

The style of language that you use depends on the type of letter you are writing. The servant in the example above would not use formal, complex language – you would write this letter in simple, everyday language. (You may have to do some research into the kind of language used by the Victorians, too!)

The language you use must be **consistent** throughout the letter. Don't lapse into your normal language halfway through.

Here is the beginning of the letter:

73 Cheyne Walk
Suffolkton
The first of May, 1874

My dear Mama and Papa

I am writing this letter to you in my tiny attic room here at the family's town residence. Forgive me if my writing is unclear to you. My fingers are blistered and cold and I am so tired, having to get up at five to start preparing the children's breakfasts ...

ACTION to TAKE

If the idea appeals to you, why not try to finish this letter off?

The ground rules for writing and the key skills needed to write a diary, a poem, a drama or a biography are similar to the rules and skills covered above.

WRITING FOR YOUR FOLIO

Your folio contains **two** pieces of Writing:

- **one** must either convey information or be discursive (i.e. one must be transactional)
- **the other** must either describe a personal experience or be an imaginative essay in a specific literary form (i.e. the other must be expressive).

Check it

Check back to pages 4–6 for more information about your folio and page 42 for more information about the four types of Writing.

WRITING IN THE EXAM

Your end-of-course Writing exam paper lasts 1 hour 15 minutes. All candidates sit the same paper. The paper will have approximately 20 topics from which you choose **one**. Some of these will have pictures or photographs to get you thinking and give you some ideas.

Writing Exam Skills

In the exam:

- **attempt only one essay**
- **choose your essay carefully.**

Attempt only one essay

Remember, attempt only **one** essay from the selection on offer. Don't worry – you will always find one that you are able to do!

Choose your essay carefully

Choose your essay carefully.

- For example, if there is an essay about how the media affects everyday life, it would not be sensible for you to try it unless
  - you have previously thought a lot about this subject
  - you have done some research and therefore have some facts and statistics to use
  - you are good at discursive writing.
- If there is an essay about your personal experience of raising money for charity and
  - you have done this
  - you can remember lots of details and feelings about the experience
  - you are good at personal experience writing

then this is the one for you to go for!

One thing to be cautious about is tackling transactional writing in the exam. Transactional writing (writing to convey information and discursive writing) requires you to know or find out a great deal of information about a topic. If you have already done a lot of research into a certain subject and have all the information 'in your head', you may feel confident about writing a transactional essay. Otherwise, it is probably safer to try expressive writing.

Practising your Writing Exam Skills

ACTION to TAKE

Study the four essay titles on page 61. They come from a previous Writing exam. Remember to study the accompanying photograph to start you thinking. As you read through the questions, see if you can work out which type of writing each question is asking for. Is it

- **writing to convey information**
- **discursive writing**
- **personal experience writing**
- **imaginative writing in a specific literary form?**

If you are not sure, read the hints below.

Hints on choosing a question

Take your time as you go through the paper. Mark the topics which appeal to you as you read through. Then go back and think hard about which is the **best** topic for you.

- **Question 14** is asking you to write a **discursive** essay in which you have to argue that people who participate in dangerous activities (e.g. dangerous sports) should not expect the emergency services to save them. Attempt this kind of essay only if you are very knowledgeable about the subject.

- **Question 15** is asking you to write a **personal experience** essay. If you have never been on this kind of holiday, do not attempt it. If you have, to achieve a good grade you must not only describe where you went and what you did but also write about your personal feelings at the time and on reflection afterwards.

- **Question 16** is asking you to write an **imaginative** essay in the specific literary form of a short story. There are plenty of possibilities here – drawing a mind map with 'leadership' at the centre would be a good starting point. Again, to achieve a good grade, you must show that you have understood and can use all the conventions of the short story.

- **Question 17** is asking you to write an essay in which you **convey information** on the topic of your hopes and aims in life. Only attempt this essay if you have thought deeply about your ambitions and if you can write at length about them without rambling! Remember that effective writing always has a structure, even if this is as basic as beginning, middle and end.

You can see that the four different types of writing are all represented here.

The exam paper will have plenty of all four types of essay from which to choose.

By following the advice given in this chapter – and by practising writing often – you can approach any writing task with confidence.

FIRST **Look at the picture below.**

NEXT Think about people and challenges.

WHAT YOU HAVE TO WRITE

14. "Those who work in the emergency services should not have to risk their lives to rescue people who take part in dangerous activities."

Discuss this point of view.

OR

15. "A holiday with a difference."

Write about an activity holiday you have taken part in.

OR

16. **Write a short story** in which leadership plays an important part.

OR

17. In search of …

Write about what **you** are looking and hoping for from life.

WRITING CHECKLIST

Use this checklist to assess each piece of writing you do at school and at home. Fill in the boxes against each question. Use a tick or a cross to show what you have or have not done. Alternatively, ask your teacher or a friend to complete the boxes.

	Excellent	Good	OK	Try harder next time!
For every type of writing:				
Is your **vocabulary** accurate?				
Is your **paragraphing** accurate?				
Is your piece of writing **clearly structured**?				
Is your **sentence construction** accurate?				
Is your **meaning** clear at first reading?				
Is your **length** appropriate to the task?				
In writing to convey information:				
Have you shown **knowledge** of the subject?				
Have you selected **appropriate** information?				
Have you emphasised the **most important** information?				
In discursive writing:				
Have you clearly stated your **point of view**?				
Have you included **ideas** and **evidence** in support of your argument?				
Are these ideas **complex**?				
Have you been **objective**?				
Have you made **generalisations**?				
Have you **evaluated** the arguments?				
In personal experience writing:				
Have you shown **insight** into the situation?				
Have you shown **self-awareness**?				
Have you expressed your **feelings** and **reactions** sensitively?				
In imaginative writing:				
Does your writing show **imagination**?				
Have you shown skill in using the **conventions** of the chosen genre?				
Have you used **language** for effect?				

TALKING

Individual Talk

Group Discussion

Talking Checklists

The two types of talking for Standard Grade English are Individual Talk and Group Discussion. Let's start with Individual Talk.

INDIVIDUAL TALK

An individual talk is a talk given by you to an audience. Your audience could be a group in your class, the PTA, a teacher and some students or a couple of school friends.

Practise your Talk

Remember that practising really will develop your talking skills. Get everyone involved. What about asking someone at home or a friend at school to listen to your talk? You could also practise by talking in front of a mirror or by taping your talk.

The more often you practise, the better your talk will be.

ACTION to TAKE

Ask your friends or family to use the checklists on pages 74–76 to help you develop your talking skills.

Preparing and Planning

KEY SKILLS

When preparing and planning your Individual Talk:

- **don't panic!**
- **choose a topic about which you are confident**
- **know your purpose**
- **know your audience**
- **do research**
- **make notes about your topic.**

Don't panic!

Most people get nervous when they have to speak in front of others. Your talk does not have to be a formal speech – you don't have to say *Good evening, ladies and gentlemen*. You could just say *Hello* and introduce yourself.

Choose a topic about which you are confident

It may be that your teacher has given you a subject but you may also have been given a free choice. If you have a choice, it is best to choose something you know about or something you have experienced. This way, you will feel more confident.

Know your purpose

You must be clear about the purpose of your talk – just as you must be clear about the purpose of your writing.

Are you trying

- to entertain your audience?
- to persuade them about an issue?
- to reflect on something you have done?
- to put forward your views?
- to give your audience information?
- to make your audience laugh?

Remember that a talk can have lots of different purposes. You may want to persuade your audience **and** make them laugh.

Be clear in your own mind about what your purposes are before you start.

Know your audience

The audience for your writing is anyone who reads it. The audience for your talk is anyone who listens to it. The only difference is that your audience for your talk will be right in front of you, looking at you!

Find out in advance who the audience will be. If you are speaking to a class of primary children about what secondary school is like, you will have to use very simple language that they will understand. If you are talking about computer games to your computing class, you could use more complicated words that they will understand. If you gave the same talk to your French class who know nothing about computers, you would use simpler words and ideas.

Do research

If you are talking about a sport or some other information topic, do lots of research. Find books about it, surf the net and talk to people interested in the same subject.

If the subject of your talk is, for example, *My Best Holiday Ever*, then before your talk you should think about what you did and why the holiday was so good. Research this subject by asking the people who went with you for their opinions.

Make notes about your topic

Once you have chosen your topic and done some research into it, your next step is to make some notes about it.

You shouldn't write your notes in sentences – just use key words and phrases. Remember that you should never write out your whole talk or just read out an essay you have written for English or another subject. You will get no grade for doing that!

Linear form and **spider diagrams** are two useful ways of making notes. However, you may prefer making notes in a different way. Use whichever way works best for you!

- **Linear Form**

  Here are some notes for a talk explaining how I learned to play the violin – these notes are set out in linear form:

VIOLIN

First lessons – excited, teacher Miss Gibbons, horrible noise!
Practice at home – every night, three notes, Dad went to pub
Next lessons – a few more notes, teacher encouraging
School band – joined band, one of best players, felt good
Lessons – for whole year, what an improvement
Now – still learning, want to be violin teacher

Did you notice that these are not written in sentences? They are just words and phrases to jog my memory. Put your ideas down on a small piece of card (a prompt card) like this so that you can glance at it during your talk. Don't forget – your notes are just reminders for what you want to say.

- **Spider diagram**

  You could set out your notes in a spider diagram (instead of linear form) – you put your topic in the centre of the page and set out your ideas round it.

  This example is for a talk about my pet rabbit:

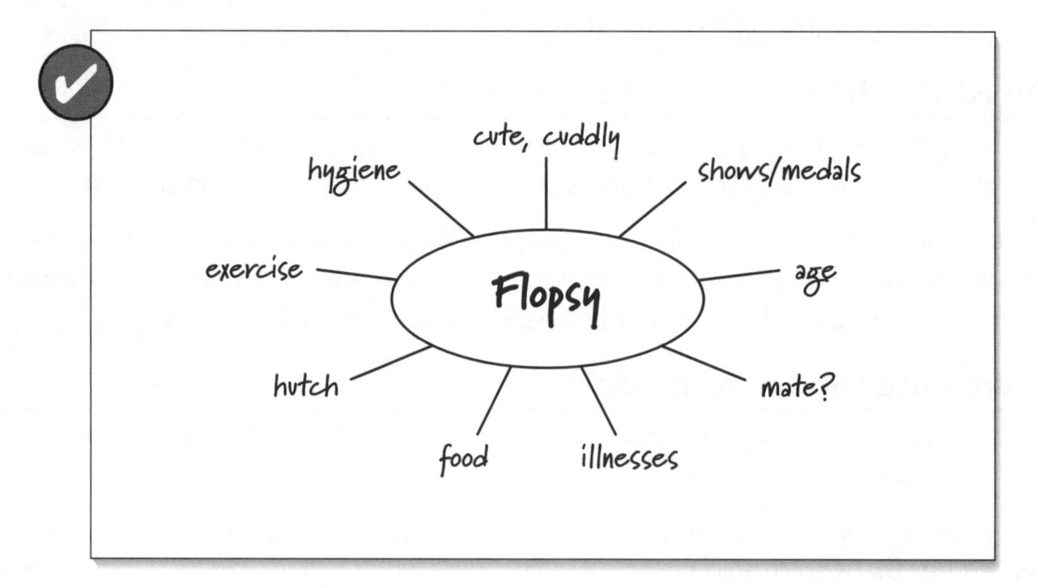

Deciding on your Content

KEY SKILLS

When deciding on the content of your Individual Talk, remember to:

- **include reasons**
- **be relevant and interesting**
- **organise your talk**
- **vary your language**
- **remember your audience**
- **use visual aids.**

Include reasons

The content of your talk refers to the ideas you include. For example, in a talk about your holiday in Florida, you will not impress anyone by saying:

Florida is awful.

You will do much better if you explain exactly what you find awful about Florida and give your reasons:

I cannot understand why anyone likes Florida. My holiday there was awful – we queued for hours at Disneyworld, we got sunstroke from the heat and, to cap it all, my dad had his wallet stolen. The hotel was dirty, there were cockroaches in the shower and ...

Be relevant and interesting

Your ideas must also be relevant: don't change the subject in the middle of your talk; do make sure all your ideas are about the topic you have chosen. Make your ideas interesting to listen to. Look back at the two Florida examples above – which one sounds more interesting to you?

Organise your talk

Always bear your purpose in mind.

- If you are conveying information, organise your talk carefully and make sure the audience is clear which information is most important.
- If you are giving a talk on a subject about which people disagree, put your ideas in a sensible order and use evidence for each of your arguments.
- If you are describing a personal experience, organise your talk into a good order. Don't ramble. Explain your feelings and reactions.

- If you are telling a story, organise your talk into a good order, use **intonation** and timing to good effect, choose your words carefully and describe the characters involved.

Vary your language

Vary the language you use in your talk – **try not to repeat words or phrases**. Think of the best words to describe something – not just the first ones that come into your head! Don't start every sentence in the same way, e.g. don't say

and don't make every sentence sound the same, e.g. don't say

Remember your audience

The language you use in everyday speech may not be appropriate for a formal talk in the classroom. Think about the kind of words you want to use – if you are talking to young children, it might be better to start your talk with

rather than

Register refers to the form of language used in certain circumstances. You should use a register appropriate to your topic and your audience. If you live in an area where a dialect is used and where everyone in the audience understands these words, it would be appropriate to include them in your speech.

Use visual aids

You don't have to use **visual aids** (e.g. pictures, diagrams on an overhead projector, photographs and demonstrations) but they almost always improve a talk. If you are talking about a famous painter whom you admire, the audience will appreciate seeing examples of his/her work. If your talk is about your favourite pop group, bring in a poster of the band. As always, think beforehand about what you could use, and take time before your talk starts to set up any charts, posters, etc.

Working on your Presentation

A great talk does not happen by accident or just because you have done a lot of practice. The presentation of your talk is very important.

For your presentation to succeed you must:

- **be expressive**
- **be aware of your audience**
- **make your talk the right length.**

Be expressive

- **Be clear**

  Being expressive means that your voice must be **clear** and your audience must be able to **hear** you. If you are softly spoken, you could practise trying to project your voice more. Often, the reason for not being audible and clear is nervousness. The more you practise, the more relaxed and confident you will be. A glass of water beside you can help – it will keep your throat clear and give you an excuse to pause and gather your thoughts!

- **Be fluent**

  Being expressive also means being fluent. If you hesitate and stumble over your words sometimes, here are two pieces of advice:

  - **practise reading out aloud**. You can choose anything to read – perhaps part of a favourite book. Read the same part over and over again if you want – this is simply an exercise to get you reading clearly and without pausing. Why not have someone to listen to you and tell you how clear you are?
  - **practise using notes** when you give a speech. Your notes should contain headings so there will be no need to pause and think 'What was I going to talk about next?' You will have noted this down and you need only glance at your notes to know what to say.

- **Adjust your pace**

  Being expressive also means adjusting the **pace** of your talk. Pace means the speed at which you speak. If you are retelling a funny experience you have had, you may feel comfortable speaking quite fast, as you would if you were telling a friend about the event. This helps to convey your excitement and enthusiasm to the audience. However, if you are giving a talk on a very complicated computer game, you may wish to speak more slowly, for example, when explaining technical words.

- **Use intonation**

  Being expressive also includes using **intonation**. This means making some words louder than others or raising the pitch of your voice. We often use loud intonation to stress an important word or phrase. We often use rising intonation at the end of a question. Think about using intonation to make your talk sound more interesting.

Be aware of your audience

- **Don't panic**

  During your talk, you must take into account the fact that you are speaking to an audience. It may be a group of your fellow students or your whole class, and other people may also be invited along – as well as, of course, your teacher. Some students find this the worst part of giving a talk, but if you have researched, prepared and practised enough, you have nothing to worry about. Remember also that it is natural to feel a little nervous in front of others. Even the most famous public speakers worry about making mistakes!

- **Look at your audience**

  Always try to look at your audience. This is one of the hardest things to do if you are nervous. If you have difficulty looking at your audience, a handy hint is to look at a point just above their faces.

- **Make eye contact**

  Make eye contact with members of the audience and give them something interesting to look at. If your face remains the same and your eyes are lowered, your audience will quickly lose interest in listening to you. You could also use your hands to emphasise important points or to show or point to visual aids.

- **Respond to your audience**

  If your audience laughs at a joke you make, pause before you go on. If your audience contains young children, keep your language and ideas simple. If your audience are already experts on the topic of your talk, don't bore them with information they already know.

- **Keep going**

  Always try to keep going. There is nothing worse than 'going blank' in front of an audience, or forgetting what you were going to say or stopping before the end. Your teacher or a member of the audience will then have to prompt you with a question. If you have prepared your notes and have practised in front of family or friends, this is much less likely to happen.

Make your talk the right length

Your teacher may suggest a length for your talk – say, two or three minutes. In this case, it is important to keep your talk going for the agreed time. If you have not been given a time, then **think about how much you want to say**. If you are giving a talk about your work experience at a children's nursery, think about headings for your talk (e.g. location, staff, accommodation, daily activities, children, your feelings during and after the experience). Think of all the details you could include under each heading (e.g. under 'children', you could describe the ages, appearance and behaviour of the children you were looking after. You could talk about your favourite child and the naughtiest child). The more details you include, the longer your talk will be.

Check it

Finally, check over the DOs and DON'Ts for your Individual Talk on page 71.

Now all you have to do is present your talk. Good luck!

DOs and DON'Ts

In each of your Individual Talks:

- ✗ **don't read out a talk you have written. This is counted as reading and not talking!**
- ✗ **don't memorise your whole talk. Again, this is counted as reading and you will get no marks.**
- ✔ **use notes (e.g. prompt cards) to help you to deliver your talk.**
- ✔ **do relax and enjoy your talk. Remember that you know more about your talk than anyone else, so be confident.**
- ✔ **do use visual aids to make your talk come alive. For example, if you are talking about a holiday, show some photos. If you are talking about a competition, bring the medal you won. If you are giving a talk about motorbikes, use an overhead projector to show a diagram of an engine.**

GROUP DISCUSSION

A group discussion is a group of two or more people discussing a topic. Usually, there are three or four members in the group. Some group members may take on the specific roles of chairperson, secretary and reporter.

SKILLS

In your Group Discussions, you should:

- **be prepared**
- **be sure of your role**
- **listen carefully to others**
- **contribute ideas and make responses to others' ideas**
- **take account of others**
- **be aware of the situation**
- **control your expression.**

Be prepared

The key to a good group discussion is preparation. You must find out about the topic before you share your ideas with others. This is true whatever the topic of your group discussion. If you are discussing a character from a novel you have read in class, it is important that you have thought about the character. If you are discussing whether the National Lottery is a good idea, you must consider all the arguments for and against. If you are discussing nuclear weapons, you could search the Internet to find some up-to-date information.

You can refer to notes during your discussion if you want, so take some notes when you find helpful information.

Don't forget that friends and family always have opinions, so ask for their ideas, too!

Be sure of your role

During the discussion itself, you may be asked to take on a specific role. The main roles are:

- **Chairperson**

  The chairperson **leads the discussion**. This means that the chairperson has several responsibilities. He/she:
  - introduces the topic
  - makes sure everyone in the group is encouraged to contribute to the discussion, especially quieter members
  - makes sure no-one speaks too much, by stopping members interrupting each other and by giving all members the opportunity to speak
  - keeps the group on task, asking questions which will help the group to move the discussion along
  - rounds off, or sums up, the discussion at the end.

  As well as all this, the chairperson contributes ideas to the group just as the other members do.

- **Secretary**

  The secretary
  - **makes notes** about the discussion
  - does **not** write **everything** down
  - **summarises** what is said using headings to organise his/her notes.

- **Reporter**

  The reporter
  - **reports back** on behalf of the group to another student, another group, the teacher or the whole class after the discussion has ended
  - gives the audience a brief summary of the group's discussion and final decisions
  - must speak clearly
  - does not add his/her own ideas to the report as he/she is speaking on behalf of the group.

Listen carefully to others

Listen to what others in your group are saying. If you do not listen carefully, you will not be able to respond – either to challenge or to agree. Other members of the group may have spent some time preparing what they have to say. It is good manners to listen to their ideas.

Contribute ideas and make responses to others' ideas

To do well in a group discussion, you must contribute a lot of ideas and make responses. This means you have responsibility for giving new ideas to the group but you must also respond to what others say.

If you say what your opinion is, you must back this up with evidence. For example, in a discussion about divorce, you could say that you feel couples should not divorce if they have children because this will cause the children a great deal of upset.

It is not enough only to contribute ideas to the discussion… you must also question and answer. If someone asks a question, try to respond to it. Alternatively, you could ask someone a question if you are unclear about what they are saying.

Take account of others

Let's look at the different ways you can take account of others in a group discussion. You can:

- **analyse** what others say. This means you examine and explore exactly what has been said.
- **summarise** what others say. This means you explain briefly the main points of the discussion, without giving extra details.
- **expand** on what others say. This means you develop ideas stated by other members of the group.
- **support** others. This means you agree with what someone has said. For example, you could use body language (such as nodding your head or smiling) or simply say

- **challenge** others. This means you disagree with what someone has said. For example, you could say

- **refute** others' ideas. This means you disagree with what someone has said and give reasons for this, for example,

It is important to remember that you have to do several of these things to gain a Credit award – not just one or two.

Be aware of the situation

If you are in a group where there is a chairperson, you must show that you are aware of this. The **chairperson** is in charge of the group, so make sure you listen to him/her (for example, you should answer if he/she asks you a question).

It is important that you **let others have their say**. Think hard about how much you speak in the group – maybe you are saying too much!

If you are aware that others in the group are quiet and have not spoken, ask a simple question to encourage them, for example,

Use language which is appropriate to the situation. If your Head Teacher is a member of the group, you might want to be more formal than usual. If the group is made up of friends you have known for a long time, your language could be more informal.

Control your expression

You must **ensure that your voice can be heard** and is clear. There is little point in preparing well and thinking of interesting contributions, if they cannot be heard in the group!

Try to **adjust the pace** of your contributions – this means the speed at which you speak. If you are making a complicated point, you might speak more slowly, for example.

Using **intonation** means making some words louder than others or raising the pitch of your voice. You could use loud intonation to stress an important word or phrase. You could use rising intonation at the end of a question. Think about using intonation when you contribute to the discussion.

TALKING CHECKLISTS

Use these checklists to assess your talking. Fill in the boxes against each question. Use a tick or a cross to show what you have or have not done. Alternatively, ask your teacher or a friend to complete the boxes.

Individual Talk Checklist

Content	Excellent	Good	OK	Try harder next time!
Did your talk contain interesting ideas?	☐	☐	☐	☐
Did your talk contain relevant ideas?	☐	☐	☐	☐
Were your ideas linked to each other?	☐	☐	☐	☐

Individual Talk Checklist (cont.)

	Excellent	Good	OK	Try harder next time!
Purpose				
In a talk to give information:				
Was there plenty of information?	☐	☐	☐	☐
Did you make clear what the most important information was?	☐	☐	☐	☐
In a talk giving a point of view:				
Were the arguments in a clear order?	☐	☐	☐	☐
Was there plenty of evidence for what you said?	☐	☐	☐	☐
In a talk giving an account of a personal experience:				
Did your audience understand your account?	☐	☐	☐	☐
Did you explain your feelings?	☐	☐	☐	☐
Did you explain your reactions?	☐	☐	☐	☐
In a talk which tells a story:				
Did you organise your story into a clear order?	☐	☐	☐	☐
Did you use the right tone?	☐	☐	☐	☐
Did you use good timing?	☐	☐	☐	☐
Did you use interesting words?	☐	☐	☐	☐
Did you describe the people in your story?	☐	☐	☐	☐
Language				
Did you use a variety of interesting words?	☐	☐	☐	☐
Did you use different types of sentence?	☐	☐	☐	☐
Did you use language suitable for your audience?	☐	☐	☐	☐
Expression				
Could your audience hear you?	☐	☐	☐	☐
Was your voice clear?	☐	☐	☐	☐
Did you hesitate or stumble over words?	☐	☐	☐	☐
Did you vary the speed of your speaking?	☐	☐	☐	☐
Did you use intonation to make your talk interesting?	☐	☐	☐	☐
Awareness of audience				
Were you aware of your audience?	☐	☐	☐	☐
Did you look at your audience?	☐	☐	☐	☐
Did you use your hands and face?	☐	☐	☐	☐
Did you need to be helped to continue?	☐	☐	☐	☐
Duration				
Did you talk for a suitable length of time?	☐	☐	☐	☐

Turn to next page for the **Group Discussion Checklist**. ▷▷

Group Discussion Checklist

	Excellent	Good	OK	Try harder next time!
Contributions				
Did you provide a good number of relevant ideas or opinions?	☐	☐	☐	☐
Did you support these ideas with evidence?	☐	☐	☐	☐
Did you question and answer relevantly?	☐	☐	☐	☐
Account of others				
Did you analyse/summarise/use/expand/support/challenge/refute the ideas of others?	☐	☐	☐	☐
Awareness				
Did you acknowledge the status of the chairperson, secretary and reporter?	☐	☐	☐	☐
Did you allow or encourage others to speak?	☐	☐	☐	☐
Did you speak readily but not too much?	☐	☐	☐	☐
Did you use language suited to your listeners?	☐	☐	☐	☐
Expression				
Were you audible and clear?	☐	☐	☐	☐
Did you use intonation?	☐	☐	☐	☐
Specific roles				
Chairperson:				
Did you introduce the topic for discussion?	☐	☐	☐	☐
Did you encourage everyone to contribute?	☐	☐	☐	☐
Did you control members of the group?	☐	☐	☐	☐
Did you keep everyone on task?	☐	☐	☐	☐
Did you round off the discussion?	☐	☐	☐	☐
Secretary:				
Did you make notes of the discussion?	☐	☐	☐	☐
Did you select key ideas?	☐	☐	☐	☐
Did you summarise the discussion?	☐	☐	☐	☐
Reporter:				
Did you report back effectively?	☐	☐	☐	☐
Did your report contain a summary of the discussion?	☐	☐	☐	☐
Did you reflect on the ideas of the group?	☐	☐	☐	☐
Were you audible?	☐	☐	☐	☐
Were you clear?	☐	☐	☐	☐

KEY WORDS

Key Words

action	what happens in a text (sometimes called the plot or narrative)
alliteration	repetition of the same letter or sound at the beginning of words, e.g. 'Round and round the ragged road, the ragged rascal ran.'
analysis	an explanation of why a writer has written in a certain way
argue	to state the arguments for or against a case
audience	people who read a text or listen to a presentation
authorial stance	the writer's point of view
chairperson	the leader in a group discussion
challenge	to question what another person thinks or says
character	a person in a text
cinematography	the use of the camera in film-making
colloquial	ordinary, informal (words and phrases)
conclusion	the ending of a piece of writing
connotation	the association connected with a particular word or phrase
content	the ideas contained in a text
continuous assessment	regular marking of students' work in class
conventions	the aspects found in a particular literary form
craft	the writer's technique
critical evaluation	an essay which judges the success of a particular text
deploy ideas	to explain ideas in support of an argument
description	the words a writer uses to describe a place, an event, a character, etc.
dialect	words and phrases used in a particular geographical area, e.g. Scotland
dialogue	conversation between characters
direction	instructions given by a director to an actor
duration	length
edit	to prepare a film by rearranging, selecting, changing
elements	in Standard Grade English, the parts of the course
evaluate	to judge the worth of a text or argument
evidence	proof from a text in the form of quotations or points
expand	to increase a number of ideas
expound	to explain an argument in detail
expression	the choice of words and phrases used by a writer
expressive	explaining feelings
eye contact	looking at the listener during a talk

fact	a true statement or account
fiction	writing which is imaginary
figures of speech	phrases in which the meaning is not literal, e.g. 'Her eyes twinkled like diamonds.'
folio	in Standard Grade English, a collection of five pieces of writing
formal language	language which follows precise conventions and is grammatically correct with no abbreviations
genre	a type of text
grade-related criteria	the standards against which work is marked
imagery	descriptive words or phrases containing figures of speech
imaginative response	a piece of writing based on a text the writer has read and appreciated, using its ideas and mood
informal language	everyday language which may not be grammatically precise and includes abbreviations and tags such as 'ya know' and 'I mean'
intonation	variation in the sound of a voice
introduction	the first section of a piece of writing
language	the words and phrases used in a text
layout	the arrangement of writing on the page
lighting	the use of light in film-making
linear form	notes written in lines
linking	how a passage of writing is connected together
main body	the middle section of a piece of writing
metaphor	a comparison between two things which is not literal, for example, 'He was a lion in battle.'
mind map	a method of brainstorming connected ideas (similar to a spider diagram)
mise en scène	every aspect within a shot in film-making, including scenery, lighting, acting, props, costumes …
mood	the atmosphere or feeling of a text
narrative	what happens in a text (sometimes called the plot or the action)
narrative voice	the point of view used in a text
non-fiction	writing which is factual
pace	speed
personification	description of an animal or object as though it is human, for example, 'The car's headlights blinked.'
plot	what happens in a text (sometimes called the action or narrative)
purpose	the reason a text is written

redrafting	improving a piece of writing by rewriting
reflective writing	writing in which the writer considers his/her feelings
refute	to prove an argument is wrong
register	a form of language, for example, journalese
reporter	the member of a group discussion who summarises what the group has said for the benefit of others
representation	characterisation in films, television and the media
rhyme	in poetry, words which have the same endings
rhythm	in poetry, the arrangement of lines into short and long beats
salutation	'Dear …' at the beginning of a letter
secretary	the member of a group discussion who takes notes of what is said
setting	in a piece of writing, the time and place of the action
simile	a comparison between two things which is not literal, using 'like' or 'as', for example, 'He was like a lion in battle.'
skimming	quick reading to get the gist of a text
sound	any sound in film, television or radio, e.g. music, voices, sound effects
specific literary form	a type of writing with certain conventions (e.g. a novel, a letter, a diary, a poem, a script)
spider diagram	a method of brainstorming connected ideas (similar to a mind map)
stage directions	instructions to actors about how they should move, speak, etc.
structure	the order and organisation of a text
style	a combination of the language, structure, imagery, and content a writer uses
summarise	to condense into a shortened form
support	to use evidence to back up a point or argument
technique	a method used by a writer to create a style
theme	the underlying 'message' of a text
tone	tone in writing is the same as tone of voice, e.g. angry, sarcastic, sympathetic
transactional writing	functional writing which aims to get something done, e.g. a letter of complaint
unit	in Standard Grade English, one part of the course, e.g. a lesson or series of lessons
verse	a group of lines in a poem (sometimes called a 'stanza')
visual aids	pictures or objects used for illustration in a talk